PRAYERS
for
PEACE

PRAYERS
for
PEACE

Δ

*An anthology of readings and prayers
selected by Archbishop Robert Runcie
and Cardinal Basil Hume*

First published in Great Britain February 1987
Second impression March 1987
SPCK
Holy Trinity Church
Marylebone Road
London NW1 4DU

British Library Cataloguing in Publication Data

Prayers for peace: an anthology of readings and prayers.
1. Prayer-books
I. Runcie, Robert   II. Hume, George Basil
242'.8   BV245

ISBN 0-281-04265-9

Printed in Great Britain by
Hazell Watson & Viney Limited,
Member of the BPCC Group,
Aylesbury, Bucks

I

Conflict and Division

It is quite clear that where our Lord is, peace reigns and anger has no place. I could see no sort of anger in God, however long I looked. Indeed, if God were to be angry but for a moment we could not live, endure, or be! Just as we owe our existence to God's everlasting might, wisdom and goodness, so by these same qualities are we kept in being. And though we wretches know from our own experience the meaning of discord and tension, we are still surrounded in every conceivable way by God's gentleness and humility, his kindness and graciousness. I saw quite clearly that our eternal friendship, our continuing life and existence is in God.

The same eternal goodness that keeps us from perishing when we sin keeps on giving a peace which offsets our own anger and wrong-headed falling. It makes us realize with a genuine dread what is our real need; it urges us strongly to seek God and his forgiveness; by God's grace it makes us want salvation. We cannot be safe and happy until we know real love and peace: that is what salvation is. Even if we, through our own anger and wrong-headedness, do have to go through hardship and discomfort and trouble, which are the outcome of our blind weakness, we are still kept safe and sound by the mercy of God, so that we do not perish. But there will be no joyful salvation or eternal happiness until we are completely at peace and in love. In other words, until we are wholly content with God, his actions, and decisions; until we are in love and at peace with ourselves, our fellow Christians, and with all that God loves. Love is like that. And it is God's goodness that effects this in us.

Julian of Norwich

Often we are in tumult . . . That is why our prayer is trembling and hesitant, a prayer of tumult, uncertainty and incoherence . . .

Instead of seeking to share God's serenity, we ask God to share our tumult. Of course he does share it, but with his own serenity. This turmoil, disorder, disharmony, discord often enter our lives both in us and around us. They are caused by events we do not understand and human actions which are also tormented. And this is the essential problem, the link between the turmoil of life and our prayer, disturbance and serenity. We must realize in advance that in every confrontation between our inner peace and the hurly-burly of life, victory will go to the turmoil, because our prayer is weak and life is hard. Life is ruthless whereas our prayer, our inner peace and serenity is fragile. If we want to keep it and gain the victory over life, this must not be by open confrontation but as water waters the earth. The Fathers said that water is an image of humility. It goes to the bottom. This is quite true, but water is also invincible. When through its weight it reaches the bottom, it begins to rise and nothing can stop it. This is what our prayer should do.

Anthony Bloom

The life of Christian discipleship is one of a constant tension between 'desert' and 'market place'. 'Desert' in this context means a place where we can withdraw to be alone with God . . .

The essence of the desert is that one is alone and therefore exposed to the silence of God, that scary creative silence that provides the optimal conditions for a man's encounter with his maker. The 'market place' is, quite simply, where the people are, where life throbs and where the cries of the joyous and the desolate fill the air. Here we meet with God incarnate, God made man, made you, made me, made neighbour. God is everywhere; his glory fills the desert and he walks beside us in the market place . . . The tension between the call to the desert and to the market place arises not from the greater presence of God in one or the other but from our varying psychological needs to apprehend him in different ways.

An understanding of this tension in ourselves and the acceptance of it as an integral part of life is of fundamental importance in achieving that vital peace of soul without which life becomes a torment. When we dwell in the desert we live with the painful awareness of the sick in need of a doctor, of the imprisoned in need of a liberator, of the indifferent in need of awakening. And yet when, made desperate by the cries of those who need our help, any man's help, we leave the desert and go into the market place, it is not long before we find that both our desire and our power to serve have been generated in the periods of aloneness and silence. Desert or market place, it is not a question of pitching our tent in one or the other, but of learning to go forth and withdraw as the needs of our brother and the needs of our spirit demand.

Sheila Cassidy

[89]

When the heart is hard and parched up,
  come upon me with a shower of mercy.
When grace is lost from life,
  come with a burst of song.
When tumultuous work raises its din on
    all sides, shutting me out from beyond,
  come to me, my Lord of silence,
    with thy peace and rest.
When my beggarly heart sits crouched,
    shut up in a corner,
  break open the door, my king,
    and come with the ceremony of a king.
When desire blinds the mind with delusion
    and dust,
  O thou holy One, thou wakeful,
    come with thy light and thy thunder.

Rabindranath Tagore

CONTENTS

PREFACE

The Pope's invitation to religious leaders from all over the world to join him at Assisi for a Day of Prayer for Peace was both historic and inspiring. It was certainly a day we shall never forget: united with Christians of various denominations as well as with representatives of other faiths, we came together in Assisi to pray for the cause of peace.

We have chosen this selection of readings and prayers from a variety of authors, times, places and religions because we wanted to extend the vision of Assisi. They are an invitation to Christians to join us on our pilgrimage of prayer, faith and harmony. They also provide witness from other faiths of a profound sense of the divine and of a concern for the future of humanity.

The form and content of these prayers are very different. There can be no question of reducing them to a kind of common denominator. Each individual has to follow with the utmost sincerity his or her conscience with the aim of seeking and obeying the truth. For Christians, prayer is offered to the Father through the Holy Spirit in union with the Son. The diversity of voices echoed in these pages is proof that humanity as a whole shares a longing for the Infinite and for peace on earth.

November 1986

Robert Runcie
Basil Hume

ACKNOWLEDGEMENTS

The editors and publishers would like to thank the following people and organizations for their advice and suggestions, without which the compilation of this anthology would not have been possible:

Bishop George Appleton; David Arnott (Buddhist Peace Fellowship); Revd Jack Austin (Shin Buddhist Assoc. of Great Britain); Revd R. S. Beresford (Dept. for International Affairs, Bishop's Conference of England and Wales); E. G. W. Bill (Lambeth Palace Library); Rabbi Lionel Blue; J. L. Bond (Catholic Central Library and Information Centre); Revd Marcus Braybrooke (World Congress of Faiths); Dr Sebastian Brock (Oriental Institute, Oxford); Dr Alan S. Brown (The Shap Working Party on World Religions in Education); John Careswell (Prayer for Peace); A. S. Chhatwal (The Sikh Cultural Society of Great Britain); Br Christopher, OMF (Franciscan Study Centre); Yolande Clarke (Quaker Peace and Service); Bishop Kenneth Cragg; Fr Charles A. Cesaretti (The Episcopal Church Centre, New York); Br Daniel Faivre (Westminster Interfaith Programme); Hilary Fenton (Pax Christi); Professor John Ferguson (Selly Oak Colleges, Birmingham); Revd Kenneth Fleming (Friends of the London Peace Pagoda); Rabbi Albert H. Friedlander (Leo Baeck College); Br Geoffrey, SSF (Society of St Francis); Rabbi Hugo Gryn (West London Synagogue of British Jews); Ismail Haji Abdul Halim (The Muslim College); Dr Mary Hall (Birmingham Multi-Faith Resource Unit); Revd Richard Harries (King's College London); Jillian Hewitt (Keston College); Revd Sidney Hinkes (Anglican Pacifist Fellowship); Canon Christopher Hill (Lambeth Palace); Elisabeth Holditch; Gerard W. Hughes, SJ; B. K. Sister Jayanti (Brahma Kumaris World Spiritual University); Br John-Francis, SSF (Society of St Francis); His Holiness Pope John Paul II; Carolina Kaounides (Religious Bodies Liaison Panel, Amnesty International British Section); Dr Ursula King (Dept. of Theology, University of Leeds); Mgr George Leonard (Archbishop's House,

Westminster); Helen Lidgett (Women in Interfaith Dialogue Group, British Council of Churches); Dr Denis MacEoin (Dept. of Religious Studies, University of Newcastle upon Tyne); Anne McDonagh (The Corrymeela Community, Belfast); Dr Peter McKenzie (Dept. of Religion, University of Leicester); Ronald C. Maddox (The Buddhist Society); Fr Basil Meeking (Secretariatus, Citta Del Vaticano); Peggy Morgan (The Shap Working Party on World Religions in Education); Dr Joseph Needham (East Asian History of Science Library, Cambridge); Patricia O'Callaghan (United Nations Information Centre, London); Professor Geoffrey Parrinder; Revd John Reardon (The United Reformed Church); Ghulam Sarwar (The Muslim Educational Trust); Revd David Scott; Imaduddin Ahmed Sheikh (Society for the Promotion of Qur'anic Knowledge); A. Siddiqui (The Islamic Foundation); Frank Smith (Baptist Peace Fellowship); Roy W. Smith (The General Assembly of Unitarian and Free Christian Churches); Kathryn Spink; Hannah Stanton (World Conference on Religions and Peace); Jenny Stephenson (Religious Bodies Liaison Panel, Amnesty International British Section); Swami Tripurananda (Ramakrishna Vedanta Centre); Patrick M. Victory (Archbishop's House, Westminster); Dr Philip Walters (Keston College); Revd Professor Rowan Williams (Christ Church, University of Oxford); Dr Roger Williamson (Div. of International Affairs, British Council of Churches); Canon Gordon Wilson (Week of Prayer for World Peace); Revd John Witheridge (Lambeth Palace); Vickie Wood-Jones (Dept. of Peace Studies, University of Bradford).

Special thanks are due to Frances Knight, who helped in researching and collecting material for the anthology during the early stages of its preparation.

Lead me from Death to Life

from Falsehood to Truth

Lead me from Despair to Hope

from Fear to Trust

Lead me from Hate to Love

from War to Peace

Let Peace fill our Heart

our World, our Universe

Peace   Peace   Peace

For they have healed the hurt of the
    daughter of my people slightly,
saying, Peace, peace:
when there is no peace.

Jeremiah 8.11

For thus saith the high and lofty One
    that inhabiteth eternity, whose name
    is Holy:
I dwell in the high and holy place,
    with him also that is of a contrite
    and humble spirit . . .
Peace, peace to him that is far off,
    and to him that is near,
    saith the lord;
    and I will heal him.
But the wicked are like the troubled
    sea,
    when it cannot rest,
    whose waters cast up mire and dirt.
There is no peace, saith my God,
    to the wicked.

Isaiah 57.15–21

By the snorting war-horses that strike fire with their hoofs as they storm forward at dawn, a single host in the midst of their dust cloud.

Man is indeed ungrateful to his Lord. Witness what he does. Violent is he in his passion for wealth. Are they not aware that their Lord is cognizant of everything about them on that Day when the tombs yield up their dead and all men's hidden thoughts are public knowledge?

From the Qur'an

To joy in conquest is to joy in the loss of human life.

He who joys in bloodshed is not fit to govern the country . . .

He who has occasion to kill many people has cause for deep sorrow and tears.

Lao Tzu

The Wise Lord wants man to fight against ignorance, destitution, disease and vice. It is sheer madness for man to fight against man.

War is the worst scourge that destroys men's wealth and morals.

War is the greatest crime man perpetrates against man.

Zarathustra

In this day of man's highest technical achievement, in this day of dazzling discovery, of novel opportunities, loftier dignities and fuller freedoms for all, there is no excuse for the kind of blind craving for power and resources that provoked the wars of previous generations. There is no need to fight for food and land. Science has provided us with adequate means of survival and transportation, which make it possible to enjoy the fullness of this great earth. The question now is, do we have the morality and courage required to live together as brothers and not be afraid?

One of the most persistent ambiguities we face is that everybody talks about peace as a goal, but among the wielders of power peace is practically nobody's business. Many men cry 'Peace! Peace!' but they refuse to do the things that make for peace.

The large power blocs talk passionately of pursuing peace while expanding defence budgets that already bulge, enlarging already awesome armies and devising ever more devastating weapons . . .

Before it is too late, we must narrow the gaping chasm between our proclamations of peace and our lowly deeds which precipitate and perpetuate war. We are called upon to look up from the quagmire of military programmes and defence commitments and read the warnings on history's signposts.

One day we must come to see that peace is not merely a distant goal that we seek but a means by which we arrive at that goal. We must pursue peaceful ends through peaceful means. How much longer must we play at deadly war games before we heed the plaintive pleas of the unnumbered dead and maimed of past wars?

Martin Luther King, Jr

Will It Be So Again?

Will it be so again
That the brave, the gifted are lost from view,
And empty, scheming men
Are left in peace their lunatic age to renew?
Will it be so again?

Must it be always so
That the best are chosen to fall and sleep
Like seeds, and we too slow
In claiming the earth they quicken, and the old
    usurpers reap
What they could not sow?

Will it be so again –
The jungle code and the hypocrite gesture?
A poppy wreath for the slain
And a cut-throat world for the living? that stale
    imposture
Played on us once again?

Will it be as before –
Peace, with no heart or mind to ensue it,
Guttering down to war
Like a libertine to his grave? We should not be
    surprised: we knew it
Happen before.

Shall it be so again?
Call not upon the glorious dead
To be your witnesses then.
The living alone can nail to their promise the ones
    who said
It shall not be so again.

Cecil Day Lewis

[6]

The story, Lord, is as old as history,
    as remorseless as man:
Man the raider, the plunderer, the terrorist,
    the conqueror,
Defiling the light of dawn with
The conspiracies of night,
Perverting to evil the fine instruments of nature,
Dealing fear among the tents and the homesteads
Of the unsuspecting or the weak,
Confiscating, purloining, devastating.

The passions are more subtle in our time –
The fire-power of bombs for the dust-clouds of cavalry,
Napalm and incendiary and machines in the skies,
Devices for war decrying the stars,
New skills with the same curse of destruction,
The sanctity of mankind in the jeopardy of techniques,
Gracelessness against the majesty on high.

By the truth of the eternal exposure,
By the reckoning of the eternal justice,
By compassion upon kin and kind,
By the awe of thy sovereignty,
Turn our deeds, O good Lord,
Repair our ravages,
Forgive our perversities.
O God, give peace, grateful peace.

Kenneth Cragg

Almighty and merciful God, Father of all men,
Creator and Ruler of the universe, Lord of history,
whose designs are inscrutable,
whose glory is without blemish,
whose compassion for the errors of men is inexhaustible,
in your will is our peace!
Mercifully hear this prayer
which rises to you from the tumult and desperation of a world
in which you are forgotten,
in which your name is not invoked,
your laws are derided
and your presence is ignored.
Because we do not know you, we have no peace . . .

Grant us prudence in proportion to our power,
wisdom in proportion to our science,
humaneness in proportion to our wealth and might.
And bless our earnest will to help all races and peoples to
*   travel, in friendship with us,*
along the road to justice, liberty and lasting peace:
But grant us above all to see that our ways are not necessarily
*   your ways,*
that we cannot fully penetrate the mystery of your designs
and that the very storm of power now raging on this earth
reveals your hidden will and your inscrutable decision.
Grant us to see your face in the lightning of this cosmic
*   storm,*
O God of holiness, merciful to men:
Grant us to seek peace where it is truly found!

*   In your will, O God, is our peace!*

Thomas Merton

*To you, Creator of nature and humanity, of truth and
beauty, I pray:*

*Hear my voice, for it is the voice of the victims of all
wars and violence among individuals and nations.*

*Hear my voice, for it is the voice of all children who
suffer and will suffer when people put their faith in
weapons and war.*

*Hear my voice when I beg you to instil into the hearts
of all human beings the wisdom of peace, the strength of
justice and the joy of fellowship.*

*Hear my voice, for I speak for the multitudes in every
country and in every period of history who do not want
war and are ready to walk the road of peace.*

*Hear my voice and grant insight and strength so that we
may always respond to hatred with love, to injustice with
total dedication to justice, to need with the sharing of self,
to war with peace.*

*O God, hear my voice, and grant unto the world your
everlasting peace.*

Pope John Paul II

We confess that in our lives we do not always choose the
  way of peace.
We spread gossip which fans the flame of hatred.
We are ready to make any sacrifices when Caesar
  demands – but few when God invites.
We worship the false god of security and nationalism.
We hold out one hand in friendship – but keep a weapon
  in the other behind our back.
We have divided your body of people into those we trust
  and those we do not.
Huge problems challenge us in the world – but our greed,
  fear and selfishness prevent us from uniting to solve
  them.
Lord, we need your help and forgiveness, your reconciling
  power.

Pax Christi

God of all grace, call to the nations of the earth to cease
from strife, that all may join to fight not one another but
their common foes of want and ignorance, disease and sin.

Lead back mankind out of the way of death into the
way of life; and from destruction to the building up of a
new world of righteousness and peace, of liberty and joy.

End the dark night of lies and cruelty; bring in the
dawn of mercy and of truth.

Week of Prayer for World Peace

Gracious Father,
we pray for peace in our world:
for all national leaders
that they may have wisdom to know
    and courage to do what is right;
for all men and women
that their hearts may be turned to
    yourself in the search for
    righteousness and truth;
for those who are working to improve
    international relationships,
that they may find the true way of
    reconciliation;
for those who suffer as a result of war:
    the injured and disabled,
    the mentally distressed,
    the homeless and hungry,
    those who mourn for their dead,
    and especially for those
        who are without hope or friend
        to sustain them in their grief.

Baptist Peace Fellowship

May it be your will,
O Lord our God and God of our fathers,
that you abolish wars and bloodshed from the world,
and draw down a great and wonderful peace on the world.
Let all the dwellers on earth recognize the truth
    for what it is,
namely that we have not come into this world for the sake
    of strife and conflict,
Heaven forbid,
nor for hate, jealousy, provocation, or bloodshed,
Heaven forbid,
but we have come into this world
in order to recognize you and know you.

Nahman of Bratslav

To humble beings, immersed in suffering without respite,
all harried by terrible and endless karma,[1]
unbearable disease,
fighting, starvation and all manner of dangers:
Let an ocean of happiness
and peace arise.

Dalai Lama

[1] See note 12, p.102

2

Visions of Unity

But in the last days it shall come to pass
    that the mountain of the house of the Lord
shall be established in the top of the mountains,
    and it shall be exalted above the hills;
and people shall flow unto it.
    And many nations shall come, and say,
Come, and let us go up to the mountain of the
      Lord,
    and to the house of the God of Jacob;
and he will teach us of his ways,
    and we will walk in his paths:
for the law shall go forth of Zion,
    and the word of the Lord from Jerusalem.
And he shall judge among many people,
    and rebuke strong nations afar off;
and they shall beat their swords into ploughshares,
    and their spears into pruninghooks:
nation shall not lift up sword against nation,
    neither shall they learn war any more . . .
For all people will walk
    everyone in the name of his god,
and we will walk in the name of the Lord our God
    for ever and ever.

Micah 4.1–5

Our hope as Christians is not fundamentally in man's naked good will and rationality. We believe that he can overcome the deadly selfishness of class or sect or race by discovering himself as a child of the universal God of love. When a man realizes that he is a beloved child of the Creator of all, then he is ready to see his neighbours in the world as brothers and sisters. That is one reason why those who dare to interpret God's will must never claim him as an asset for one nation or group rather than another. War springs from the love and loyalty which should be offered to God being applied to some God-substitute, one of the most dangerous being nationalism . . .

Man without God is less than man. In meeting God, a man is shown his failures and his lack of integrity, but he is also given strength to turn more and more of his life and actions into love and compassion for other men like himself. It is necessary to the continuance of life on this planet that more and more people make this discovery. We have been given the choice. Man possesses the power to obliterate himself, sacrificing the whole race on the altar of some God-substitute. Or he can choose life in partnership with God the Father of all.

Robert Runcie

Islam is an Arabic word. It is derived from two roots, one *salm*, meaning peace, and the other SLM, meaning submission. Islam stands for 'a commitment to surrender one's will to the will of God' and as such be at peace with the Creator and all that has been created by him. It is through submission to the will of God that peace is produced. Harmonization of man's will with the will of God brings about harmonization of different spheres of life under an all-embracing ideal. Departmentalization of life into different water-tight compartments, religious and secular, sacred and profane, spiritual and material, is ruled out. There is unity of life and unity of the source of guidance. As God is One and indivisible, so is life and man's personality . . .

Everything originates from the one God and everyone is ultimately responsible to him. Thus the unity of the Creator has as its corollary the oneness of his creation. Distinctions of race, colour, caste, wealth and power disappear; man's relation with fellow man assumes total equality by virtue of the common Creator.

Islamic Council of Europe

The political ideal of the world is not so much a single empire with a homogeneous civilization and a single communal will, but a brotherhood of free nations differing profoundly in life and mind, habits and institutions, existing side by side in peace and order, harmony and co-operation, and each contributing to the world its own unique and specific best, which is irreducible to the terms of the others . . .

Let us believe in a unity of spirit and not of organization, a unity which secures ample liberty not only for every individual but for every type of organized life which has proved itself effective. For almost all historical forms of life and thought can claim the sanction of experience and so the authority of God. The world would be a much poorer thing if one creed absorbed the rest. God wills a rich harmony and not a colourless uniformity. The comprehensive and synthetic spirit of Hinduism has made it a mighty forest with a thousand waving arms each fulfilling its function and all directed by the spirit of God.

Sarvepalli Radhakrishnan

Buddhism aims at creating a society where the ruinous struggle for power is renounced; where calm and peace prevail away from conquest and defeat; where the persecution of the innocent is vehemently denounced; where one who conquers oneself is more respected than those who conquer millions by military and economic warfare; where hatred is conquered by kindness, and evil by goodness; where enmity, jealousy, ill-will and greed do not infect men's minds; where compassion is the driving force of action; where all, including the least of living things, are treated with fairness, consideration and love; where life in peace and harmony, in a world of material contentment, is directed towards the highest and noblest aim, the realization of the Ultimate Truth, *Nirvana*.[2]

Walpola Rahula

[2] See note 19, p.103

The purpose of religion as revealed from the heaven of God's holy will is to establish unity and concord amongst the peoples of the world; make it not the cause of dissension and strife. The religion of God and his divine law are the most potent instruments and the surest of all means for the dawning of the light of unity amongst men. The progress of the world, the development of nations, the tranquillity of peoples, and the peace of all who dwell on earth are among the principles and ordinances of God. Religion bestoweth upon man the most precious of all gifts, offereth the cup of prosperity, imparteth eternal life, and showereth imperishable benefits upon mankind . . .

We call upon the manifestations of the power of God – the sovereigns and rulers on earth – to bestir themselves and do all in their power that haply they may banish discord from this world and illumine it with the light of concord.

Bahá'u'lláh

Since wars begin in the minds of men, it is in the minds of men that the defences of peace must be constructed.

UNESCO Constitution

Lord of all creation,
we stand in awe before you,
impelled by visions of the harmony of man.
We are children of many traditions –
inheritors of shared wisdom and tragic misunderstandings,
of proud hopes and humble successes.
Now it is time for us to meet –
in memory and truth,
in courage and trust,
in love and promise.

In that which we share,
let us see the common prayer of humanity;
in that in which we differ,
let us wonder at the freedom of man;
in our unity and our differences,
let us know the uniqueness that is God.

Forms of Prayer for Jewish Worship

We pray for all mankind.
Though divided into nations and races,
yet are all men thy children,
drawing from thee their life and being,
commanded by thee to obey thy laws,
each in accordance with the power to know and
    understand them.
Cause hatred and strife to vanish,
that abiding peace may fill the earth,
and humanity may everywhere be blessed with the fruits
    of peace.
So shall the spirit of brotherhood among men
show forth their faith that thou art the Father of all.

Liberal Jewish Prayer book

We draw near to thee who hast taught us to cast all our care on thee;
  Our Father, which art in heaven.
We are as children who have lost their way in the world's wilderness and we cry to thee;
  Our Father, which art in heaven.

Through persistent desire in all nations to seek fellowship with one another in thy one family;
  Hallowed be thy name.
Through ever-deepening aspiration towards justice, goodwill, and peace in all the world;
  Hallowed be thy name.

By the faithfulness of thy people in seeking first thy kingdom and thy righteousness;
  Thy kingdom come.
By the vindication of right and by the growth of mutual understanding between nations and races;
  Thy kingdom come.

In the maintenance of the spirit of love and equity even in the midst of strife or war;
  Thy will be done.
In the determination among all to work for secure peace in a world order that is fair to the generations yet to be;
  Thy will be done.

By co-operation among all nations and classes for the common good;
  Give us our daily bread.
By the sympathy which gives help to the needy both at home and far away;
  Give us our daily bread.

*Because by our self-interest and self-concern we have
increased the bitterness between men and between
nations;*
Forgive us our trespasses.
*Because we have trusted in our own wisdom and strength
and have neglected thee;*
Forgive us our trespasses.

*If other countries, while pursuing their own interests, have
unduly hindered ours;*
We forgive them that trespass against us.
If any have injured us by threat or by attack;
We forgive them that trespass against us.

*When opportunity comes to secure wealth for ourselves at
the cost of increased poverty to others;*
Lead us not into temptation.
*When suffering and anxiety prompt feelings of bitterness
and hatred;*
Lead us not into temptation.

*At times of self-satisfaction, self-seeking, and self-
confidence;*
Deliver us from evil.
*At times of fear concerning the designs of others and of
desire to gain security or advantage by unjust means;*
Deliver us from evil.

*For over all races and nations thou rulest as King; thy
fatherly love embraces all; and in thy will is our peace;*
Thine is the kingdom, the power, and the glory,
for ever and ever. Amen.

William Temple (adapted)

The Long Travail of Mankind

Grant us to look with your eyes of compassion,
O merciful God, at the long travail of mankind:
the wars, the hungry millions,
the countless refugees,
the natural disasters,
the cruel and needless deaths,
men's inhumanity to one another,
the heartbreak and hopelessness of so many lives.
Hasten the coming of the messianic age
when the nations shall be at peace,
and men shall live free from fear and free from want
and there shall be no more pain or tears,
in the security of your will,
the assurance of your love,
the coming of your Kingdom,
O God of righteousness, O Lord of compassion.

George Appleton

O thou whose eye is over all the children of men, and who hast called them, by thy Prince of Peace, into a kingdom not of this world; send forth his Spirit speedily into the dark places of our guilt and woe, and arm it with the piercing power of thy grace. May it reach the heart of every oppression, and make arrogancy dumb before thee.

Let it still the noise of our strife and the tumult of the people; put to shame the false idols of every mind; carry faith to the doubting, hope to the fearful, strength to the weak, light to the mourner; and more and more increase the pure in heart who see their God.

Commit thy word, O Lord, to the lips of faithful men, or the free winds of thine invisible Providence; that soon the knowledge of thee may cover the earth, as the waters cover the channels of the deep. And so let thy kingdom come, and thy will be done on earth, as it is in heaven.

James Martineau

O God!
Make good that which is between us,
unite our hearts
and guide us to paths of peace.

Anonymous (Muslim)

O God
Let us be united;
Let us speak in harmony;
Let our minds apprehend alike.
Common be our prayer;
Common be the end of our assembly;
Common be our resolution;
Common be our deliberation.
Alike be our feelings;
Unified be our hearts;
Common be our intentions;
Perfect be our unity.

From the Vedas

Let there be good to all;
Let all be free from sickness;
Let us see good and let none suffer.
Let all be happy and fearless.
Let there be sympathy for each other
and success for all work . . .
Let us all and all other beings have peace everywhere.
You are the creator and sustainer of the world.
You encourage godliness
and establish peace among the people.
Whoever is my friend today,
Let him be in peace:
Whoever is my enemy,
Let him also be in peace.

From the Vedas

Almighty God,
creator and sustainer
of all that is truly good,
destroyer of all evil:
I bring myself,
the family of mankind
and this physical world
in front of you,
and experience your healing power of love.
You, the perfect One,
are spreading rays of harmony,
peace and happiness
over me and all the world.
Your healing vision
falls on us all,
especially those in authority,
inspiring us to seek
only peace and unity
and an end to all suffering.

Anonymous (Hindu)

Loving Father,
perfect teacher,
patient guide
in these troubled times;
sitting with you,
the perfect One,
I take the influence
of your company
to teach me
the way of reconciliation,
wisdom and harmony.
I see you,
the embodiment of all solutions
for the world
and myself at this time.
Touch my heart
and my conscience daily,
that all I do
will work towards
your goal of perfection
and peace for mankind.

Anonymous (Hindu)

*As we are together, praying for Peace, let us be truly with
    each other . . .*
  Silence
*Let us be aware of the source of being common to us all
    and to all living things.*
  Silence
*Evoking the presence of the Great Compassion, let us fill
    our hearts with our own compassion – towards
    ourselves and towards all living beings.*
  Silence
*Let us pray that all living beings realize that they are all
    brothers and sisters, all nourished from the same
    source of life.*
  Silence
*Let us pray that we ourselves cease to be the cause of
    suffering to each other.*
  Silence
*Let us plead with ourselves to live in a way which will
    not deprive other living beings of air, water, food,
    shelter, or the chance to live.*
  Silence
*With humility, with awareness of the existence of life, and
    of the sufferings that are going on around us, let us
    pray for the establishment of peace in our hearts and
    on earth.*
  Amen.

Thich Nhat Hanh

We are brothers and sisters, all belonging to one great human family and are children of one Father, that art thou O Wise Lord.

Teach us to live as comrades, all in willing fellowship and loving fraternity, in brotherly helpfulness and co-operation.

Inspire us, O Wise Lord! to live in mutual understanding and trust and peace.

Zarathustra

O kind Father, loving Father, through thy mercy we have spent our day in peace and happiness; grant that we may, according to thy will, do what is right.

Give us light, give us understanding, so that we may know what pleases thee.

We offer this prayer in thy presence, O wonderful Lord:

Forgive us our sins. Help us in keeping ourselves pure. Bring us into the fellowship of those in whose company we may remember thy name . . .

May thy name forever be on the increase, and may all men prosper by thy grace.

Guru Gobind Singh

May peace reign over the earth . . .
and every ill word be driven out into the wilderness,
into the virgin forest.

Anonymous (African Traditional)

O Thou kind Lord! Thou hast created all humanity
from the same stock. Thou hast decreed that all shall
belong to the same household. In thy holy presence
they are all thy servants, gathered together at thy table
of bounty, all are illumined through the light of thy
providence.

O thou kind Lord! Unite all. Let the religions agree
and make the nations one, so that they may see each
other as one family and the whole of the earth as one
home. May they all live together in perfect harmony.

O God! Raise aloft the banner of the oneness of
mankind.
Cement thou, O God, the hearts together.

'Abdu'l-Bahá

3

The Way of Love

'He reviled me, struck me, defeated me, robbed me.' In those who harbour such thoughts hatred will never cease.

'He reviled me, struck me, defeated me, robbed me.' Those who harbour no such thoughts are free from hatred.

Hatred does not cease by hatred; hatred ceases only by love. This is the eternal law.

From the Dhammapada

Let not one deceive another nor despise any person whatever in any place. In anger or ill-will let not one wish any harm to another.

Just as a mother would protect her only child even at the risk of her own life, even so let one cultivate a boundless heart towards all beings.

Let one's thoughts of boundless love pervade the whole world – above, below and across – without any obstruction, without any hatred, without any enmity.

From the Metta Sutta

Recommendation

Promise me this day,
promise me now
while the sun is overhead
exactly at the zenith,
promise me.

Even as they
strike you down
with a mountain of hate and violence,
even as they
step on your life and crush it
like a worm,
even as they dismember, disembowel you,
remember, brother,
remember
man is not our enemy.

Just your pity,
just your hate
are invincible, limitless, unconditional.

Hatred will never let you face
the beast in man.

And one day
when you face this beast alone,
your courage intact, your eyes kind,
untroubled
(even as no one sees them),
out of your smile

will bloom a flower
and those who love you
will behold you
across ten thousand worlds of birth and dying.

Alone again
I'll go on with head bent
but knowing the immortality of love.
And on the long, rough road
both sun and moon will shine,
lightening my steps.

Thich Nhat Hanh

Ahimsa[3] is not merely a negative state of harmlessness
but it is a positive state of love, of doing good even to
the evil-doer. But it does not mean a meek submission
to the will of the evil-doer: it means the pitting of
one's whole soul against his will . . .

Mahatma Gandhi

[3] See note 37, p. 105

Love begets love and kindness begets kindness. This is a law which knows no exception. People dislike us because we have no love for them. If we love them, their love automatically flows to us. When our love goes to them and their love comes to us, the two streams mingle together and there is an ocean of love and joy. Love is not bargaining; it is not give and take. It is a spontaneous merging of souls . . .

All world-teachers unanimously declare 'O man! If you want peace for yourself and others in the world, adjust your conduct in accordance with the law of Love. Expand your vision so that it can embrace all fellow-beings and link them to yourself by Love. Rise above narrow creeds, cults, communal leanings and national ambitions. Merge your life in the infinity of God!'

Swami Ramdas

Who loves all beings without distinction,
He indeed is worshipping best his God.

Swami Vivekananda

Though our love for people must be all-inclusive, embracing the wicked as well, this in no way blunts our hatred for evil itself; on the contrary it strengthens it. For it is not because of the dimension of evil clinging to a person that we include him in our love, but because of the good in him, which our love tells us is to be found everywhere. And since we detach the dimension of the good to love him for it, our hatred for evil becomes unblunted and absolute.

It is proper to hate a corrupt person only for his defects, but in so far as he is endowed with a divine image, it is in order to love him.

Abraham Isaac Kook

If only we love the real world . . . really in its horror, if only we venture to surround it with the arms of our spirit, our hands will meet hands that grip them.

Martin Buber

But I say to you that hear, Love your enemies, do good to those who hate you, bless those who curse you, pray for those who abuse you. To him who strikes you on the cheek, offer the other also . . . If you love those who love you, what credit is that to you? For even sinners love those who love them. And if you do good to those who do good to you, what credit is that to you? For even sinners do the same. And if you lend to those from whom you hope to receive, what credit is that to you? Even sinners lend to sinners, to receive as much again. But love your enemies, and do good, and lend, expecting nothing in return; and your reward will be great, and you will be sons of the Most High; for he is kind to the ungrateful and the selfish.

Luke 6.27–35

Love is patient and kind; love is not jealous or boastful; it is not arrogant or rude. Love does not insist on its own way; it is not irritable or resentful; it does not rejoice at wrong, but rejoices in the right. Love bears all things, believes all things, hopes all things, endures all things. Love never ends.

1 Corinthians 13.4–8

Long hours of ignoble pain were a severe test. In the middle of torture they asked me if I still believed in God. When, by God's help, I said, 'I do,' they asked me why God did not save me . . .

I did not like to use the words 'Father forgive them'. It seemed too blasphemous to use our Lord's words; but I *felt* them, and I said, 'Father, I know these men are doing their duty. Help them to see that I am innocent.' When I muttered 'Forgive them', I wondered how far I was being dramatic, and if I really meant it; because I looked at their faces as they stood round, taking it in turn to flog me, and their faces were hard and cruel, and some of them were evidently enjoying their cruelty. But, by the grace of God, I saw those men not as they were, but as they had been. Once they were little children with their brothers and sisters – happy in their parent's love, in those far-off days before they had been conditioned by their false nationalist ideals. And it is hard to hate little children.

So I saw them not as they were, but as they were capable of becoming, redeemed by the power of Christ, and I knew that I should say 'Forgive'.

Leonard Wilson

When you look at someone with eyes of love, you see a reality different from that of someone who looks at the same person without love, with hatred or even just with indifference.

Desmond Tutu

May I be able to look upon all beings with the eye of a friend. May we look upon one another with the eye of a friend.

From the Vedas

Almighty God, source of true peace, as I, your child, sit in your presence absorbed in your light, I feel your loving benevolence, your deepest desire to bind and heal all the wounds of injustice, conflict and hopelessness in myself and the world. In your presence I take from you, my perfect parent, the love of peace that gives me the strength to overcome my own aggressive reactions. I take from you the vision of brotherhood of man through which I see all with that family love and respect. In seeing your perfection and your perfect vision towards me, I renounce all hatred, greed, anger and jealousy and determine to, from now on only give love to myself and the world, bringing your peace.

Anonymous (Hindu)

O Great Spirit, I pray for your blessing. I pray that you bring peace to all my brothers and sisters of this world . . . Give us the wisdom to teach our children to love, to respect, and to be kind to each other, so that they may grow with peace in mind.

Anonymous (American Indian)

May it be thy will, O Lord, that no man foster hatred against us in his heart, that we foster no hatred in our hearts against any man.

From the Talmud

O God, when I am estranged from others, when walls of misunderstanding rise between us, I fade and wither like a leaf separated from its stem. How much I need the balm of friendship, the warmth of understanding! How greatly I need to be needed and cherished! I pray therefore that my soul may know the joy of love given and received, and that no unworthiness diminish me . . .

Open my eyes to the beauty that shines within all who walk the earth. Keep me from imagined hurts, from seeing foes where only friends are to be found. And give me insight into my own heart, that I may uproot all that weakens me. Help me to be patient when others misunderstand me, open to the thoughts of those who are near to me, and quick to forgive all who wound me . . .

Anonymous (Jewish)

Lord, make our hearts abodes of peace
and our minds harbours of tranquility.
Sow in our souls true love for you and for one another
and root deeply within us friendship and unity,
and concord with reverence,
that we may give peace to each other sincerely
and receive it beautifully.

Anonymous (Christian)

The Peace Prayer of St Francis

Lord, make me an instrument of thy peace.
Where there is hatred, let me sow love.
Where there is injury, pardon.
Where there is doubt, faith.
Where there is despair, hope.
Where there is darkness, light.
Where there is sadness, joy.
O divine Master,
grant that I may not so much seek to be consoled as to
*   console;*
to be understood as to understand;
to be loved, as to love;
for it is in giving that we receive,
it is in pardoning that we are pardoned,
and it is in dying that we are born to eternal life.

Anonymous (Christian)

I offer up unto thee my prayers and intercessions, for those especially who have in any matter hurt, grieved, or found fault with me, or who have done me any damage or displeasure.

For all those also whom, at any time, I have vexed, troubled, burdened, and scandalized, by words or deeds, knowingly or in ignorance: that thou wouldst grant us all equally pardon for our sins, and for our offences against each other.

Take away from our hearts, O Lord, all suspiciousness, indignation, wrath and contention, and whatsoever may hurt charity, and lessen brotherly love.

Thomas à Kempis

O God, who hast taught us that all our doings without love are nothing worth; send down thy Holy Spirit, and pour into our hearts that most excellent gift of love, the very bond of peace and of all virtues, without which whosoever liveth is counted dead before thee; Grant this for thine only Son Jesus Christ's sake.

The Book of Common Prayer

O God we are one with you.
You have made us one with you.
You have taught us that if we are open to one another,
 you dwell in us.
Help us to preserve this openness and to fight for it
 with all our hearts.
Help us to realize that there can be no understanding
 where there is mutual rejection.
O God, in accepting one another wholeheartedly, fully,
 completely,
we accept you, and we thank you, and we adore you;
and we love you with our whole being,
 because our being is in your being,
 our spirit is rooted in your spirit.
Fill us then with love,
and let us be bound together with love as we go our
 diverse ways,
united in this one spirit which makes you present to
 the world,
and which makes you witness to the ultimate reality
 that is love.
Love has overcome.
Love is victorious.
Amen.

Thomas Merton

4

The Way of Truth

The way of peace is the way of truth . . . Truthfulness is even more important than peacefulness. Indeed, *lying is the mother of violence.* A truthful man cannot long remain violent. He will perceive in the course of his research that he has no need to be violent, and he will further discover that so long as there is the slightest trace of violence in him, he will fail to find the truth he is searching.

Mahatma Gandhi

The failure of communication which is so striking a feature of our times is based, ultimately, on a breakdown of the notion of objective truth . . .

Actual lies may not be told, but those facts which are not in accordance with the feelings and interests of this or that individual or group are increasingly ignored, misrepresented, distorted and suppressed. In extreme cases such facts are not allowed ever to have existed at all. From the stage where loyalty to the notion of objective truth becomes selective – that is to say, becomes that which is in accordance with certain personal or sectional interests – it is not a very big step to the stage where that which is in accordance with those interests becomes the truth . . .

Under these circumstances communication is impossible. Words no longer have the same meaning for everybody, and what one group regards as facts another regards as non-facts. There is a 'failure' of communication. Indeed, those whose views and attitudes are not in accordance with the interests of a particular group are treated as non-individuals in the same way that facts that are not in accordance with these same interests are regarded as non-facts. Such an individual is not so much wrong as, in theory, non-existent, and since he is non-existent in theory it is only natural that he should very quickly become non-existent in practice too.

The reinstatement of the notion of objective truth to its rightful position therefore ranks as one of our most urgent tasks. To work for the reinstatement of the notion of objective truth is, in the long run, to work for the achievement of world peace, for it is one of the most important conditions upon which the achievement of world peace depends.

Sangharakshita

'Concerning men and their way to peace and concord –?' The truth is so simple that it is considered a pretentious banality. Yet it is continually being denied by our behaviour. Every day furnishes new examples . . .

You can only hope to find a lasting solution to a conflict if you have learned to see the other objectively, but, at the same time, to experience his difficulties subjectively . . .

All first-hand experience is valuable, and he who has given up looking for it will soon find – that he lacks what he needs: a closed mind is a weakness, and he who approaches persons or painting or poetry without the youthful ambition to learn a new language and so gain access to someone else's perspective on life, let him beware.

Dag Hammarskjöld

But let us not forget that violence does not live by itself and cannot live by itself. It can only exist with the help of *the lie*. Between these two there is a most intimate, natural and fundamental connection. Violence can only be concealed by the lie, and the lie can only be maintained by violence. Any man who has once proclaimed violence as his *method* is inevitably forced to take the lie as his *principle*. When it is born, violence operates openly and even takes pride of itself. But as soon as it becomes confirmed and established, it begins to feel a thinning in the air about itself. Then it realizes it cannot carry on living except by masking itself with lies and covering itself up with sweet words. Violence does not always, not necessarily, take people by the throat and strangle them. Usually it demands no more than an oath of allegiance from its subjects. They are required merely to become accomplices in the lie.

Alexander Solzhenitsyn

No one in the world can change truth. What we can and should do is to seek truth and serve it when we have found it. The real conflict is within. Beyond armies of occupation and the hecatombs of the extermination camps, two irreconcilable enemies lie in the depths of every soul. And of what use are the victories on the battlefield if we are defeated in our innermost personal selves?

St Maximilian Kolbe

In his encyclical *Pacem in terris*, Pope John XXIII said that 'Peace must be based on truth, built on justice, supported by love and created in an atmosphere of freedom.'

In his message for the day of peace, the Holy Father, Pope John Paul II elaborates on this truth, pronounced by one of his predecessors. I want therefore to let the Holy Father, the best son of our nation, speak.

'Peace must be based on truth' (John XXIII).

'What is needed is the renewal of truth, if we are to avoid a situation where individuals, groups and nations begin to doubt the power of peace and to accept the forms of oppression. To reinstate the truth means first and foremost to call by name any act of oppression, whatever form it takes. One has to name a murder by its name – murder is always a murder; political and ideological motivation cannot change its nature . . .'

'To promote the truth as the foundation of peace means to make every endeavour to avoid the use of the lie even in a good cause. The gospel strongly underlines the link existing between the lie and violence . . . The living source of the peace of the gospel is truth. We should therefore live by truth, and then it will reveal to us unexpected lights and energies, thus opening new possibilities for peace in the world.'

Jerzy Popieluszko

Everything is changing,
nothing is our own.
Not seeing clearly,
we perpetuate the disease of the world.
May we, living rightly,
come to know Truth;
That, abiding in peace,
we may bring peace to all beings.

Anonymous (Buddhist)

May obedience conquer disobedience within this house,
and may peace triumph over discord here,
and generous giving over avarice,
reverence over contempt,
speech with truthful words over lying utterance;
may the righteous order gain the victory
over the demon of the lie.

Anonymous (Zoroastrian)

May I never cause pain to any living being.
May I never utter untruth, and . . .
May I never feel angry with the vile, the vicious
and the wrongly directed.
May there be an adjustment of things that I shall
always remain tranquil in dealing with them.

Whether people speak of me well or ill
Whether wealth comes to me or departs
Whether I live to be hundreds of thousands of years old
Or give up the spirit this day
Whether anyone holds out any kind of fears
Or with worldly riches he tempts me
In the face of all these possible things
May my footsteps swerve not from the path of truth . . .

May there be mutual love in the world.
May delusion dwell at a distance
May no one ever utter unpleasant speech
Or words that are harsh lies ensue
May all understand the Laws of Truth
and joyfully sorrow and sufferings endure.

Anonymous (Jain)

O God! purge my heart
From hypocrisy,
My conduct from dissimulation,
My tongue from falsehood,
And my eyes from treachery;
For thou indeed knowest
The treacherous glance of the eyes
And that which bosoms conceal.

Anonymous (Muslim)

Lord of peace,
be with those who guide the destinies
  of the world
so that an end may come to boasting
  and vainglory,
and the reign of arrogance dwindle in
  our time.
Give them the courage to speak the truth
and the humility to listen.
Help us all to put the good of our fellow men
above our own ambitions,
and the truth which does not profit us
above the lie which does.
So may we stand upright,
freed from the burden of fear and the weight
  of suspicion,
learning to trust each other.

Rabbi Lionel Blue

5

Justice and Reconciliation

What is it like when righteousness is the standard of conduct? The great do not attack the small, the strong do not attack the weak, the many do not oppress the few, the cunning do not deceive the simple, the noble do not despise the humble, the rich do not mock the poor, the young do not take from the old . . .

Now what is it like when force becomes the standard of conduct? The great attack the small, the strong plunder the weak, the many oppress the few, the cunning deceive the simple, the noble disdain the humble, the rich mock the poor, the young take from the old . . .

Mo Tzu

O ye who truly believe, seek your strength for defeating injustice and oppression in your steadfastness and prayers. Assuredly, God is on the side of the steadfast in truth.

From the Qur'an

Be a haven for the distressed, an upholder and defender for the victim of oppression, a home for the stranger, a balm to the sufferer, a tower to the fugitive.

Bahá'u'lláh

Blessed are the poor in spirit,
    for theirs is the kingdom of heaven.
Blessed are those who mourn,
    for they shall be comforted.
Blessed are the meek,
    for they shall inherit the earth.
Blessed are those who hunger and thirst
      for righteousness,
    for they shall be satisfied.
Blessed are the merciful,
    for they shall obtain mercy.
Blessed are the pure in heart,
    for they shall see God.
Blessed are the peacemakers,
    for they shall be called sons of God.
Blessed are those who are persecuted for
      righteousness' sake,
    for theirs is the kingdom of heaven.

Matthew 5. 3–10

If we illuminate with Christian hope those longings for justice, peace and goodness that we still have on this earth, they will be realized. Those who have put into their work a feeling of great faith, of love for God, of hope for humanity, find all that work now overflowing in the splendours of a crown. Such has been the reward for all of those who do that work, watering the earth with truth, love and kindness. These deeds are not lost; purified by the spirit of God, their effects are our reward.

Oscar Romero

Are we so deaf that we do not hear a loving God warning us that humanity is in danger of committing suicide? Are we so selfish that we do not hear the just God demanding that we do all we can to stop injustice suffocating the world and driving it to war? Are we so alienated that we can worship God at our ease in luxurious temples which are often empty in spite of all their liturgical pomp, and fail to see, hear and serve God where he is present and where he requires our presence, among mankind, the poor, the oppressed, the victims of injustices in which we ourselves are often involved?

Helder Câmara

Our generation, as never before, has been profoundly affected by the enormous disparity in wealth between the countries of the rich northern hemisphere and the developing countries of the south. Modern communications technology has brought into our living rooms sights that in the past were hidden from our view.

The misery is no longer in faraway places. It has been brought home to us. The Brandt Report some years ago warned us that time was running out and that even enlightened self-interest should lead developed countries to take radical action to redress the inequalities between north and south and to construct a more just world order . . .

Politicians tell us there are no votes in international aid. We should tell them they are wrong and that our vote would be given to enlightened policies aimed at alleviating the world's distress and injustice. We can and must still support our voluntary development and relief agencies. But we know that the problem can only be tackled by the nations working together . . .

The final horror of this century has been the appalling manifestation of man's inhumanity to man. There has been violent repression, blind hatred and inhuman cruelty. This is the century of the concentration camp and the Gulag Archipelago. This is the age of the holocaust, when racial prejudice sanctioned the massacre of millions. This is an era of official torture and terrorist violence whose innocent victims are legion . . . We have in this century seen the growth of ideologies which have reduced their opponents to sub-human status or have subjected the poor and the powerless to deprivation and exploitation . . .

Are there then no signs of hope? Is there nothing to encourage and sustain us? I believe that God's grace is inexhaustible, his life a spring which never fails. There is a yearning for peace; more and more realize that war is never the way to resolve conflict. There are signs that people are no longer prepared to tolerate injustice and deprivation for others.

Basil Hume

True reconciliation cannot take place without confrontation. Reconciliation is not feeling good; it is coming to grips with evil. In order to reconcile, Christ had to die. We must not deceive ourselves. Reconciliation does not mean holding hands and singing: 'black and white together'. It means, rather, death and suffering, giving up one's life for the sake of the other. If white and black Christians fail to understand this, we shall not be truly reconciled.

So it is with peace. One is not at peace with God and one's neighbour because one has succeeded in closing one's eyes to the realities of evil. Neither is peace a situation where terrorism of the defenceless is acceptable because it is being done under the guise of the law . . . Peace is not simply the absence of war or an uneasy quiet in the townships. Peace is the active presence of justice. It is shalom, the well-being of all.

Allan Boesak

What is to be done?

Let me then set down in summary form a few of the ways in which concerned individuals can contribute towards the global virtue of peace:

1 *Be an agent of reconciliation* in those situations of conflict which impinge on your own life – and surely nowadays almost everyone is caught up in some situation of conflict, whether international or racial or industrial or something else. But how does one help towards reconciliation in such situations? . . . What is necessary is to maintain communication. When people can talk together even about their differences, there is often remarkable progress towards a fair resolution of the conflict. On the other hand, when communication has broken down, peace has been made inaccessible . . .

2 *Be politically and socially responsible.* In the highly organized and institutionalized world in which we live, the efforts of individuals will be unavailing unless ways can be found to shape and influence the powerful and apparently depersonalized political, economic and social forces that determine the large-scale structures of human life. Most of us can find access at one point or another to organizations that have some share in shaping society . . . But to get oneself seriously involved in any of these demands time, commitment and responsibility, such as few may be willing to invest. It is so much easier to take part in a demonstration, and leave it at that! But it is only the less spectacular but steady engagement with the problems of society that will in the long run help to bring us towards a genuine peace.

3   *Exercise restraint in your material standard of living.*

Perhaps the time has come when a moderate Christian asceticism has once again an important role to play as a witness to the belief that the fullness of human life does not consist simply in the abundance of material possessions and that in any case there is something fundamentally wrong with a situation in which some people in some nations degrade themselves through over-consumption while other people in other countries are degraded by not having anything more than a marginal level of physical subsistence . . . A continuation of the present glaring inequities in the different standards of living will remain a standing threat to peace, indeed, a constant frustration of peace if we understand peace in any affirmative way . . .

4   *Pray for peace.* Though I mention this last, it is not in any sense an afterthought or an extra. Where people are praying for peace, the cause of peace is being strengthened by their very act of prayer, for they are themselves becoming immersed in the spirit of peace . . .

But to pray for peace, Christians believe, is more than just to meditate on the meaning of peace . . . It is to bring into the human situation the very power of the God of peace, or, better expressed, to open up our human situation to that power. No doubt at any given time only a tiny minority of mankind is actively praying for peace in this way. But no one can say what is being accomplished through the openings into the human situation which they provide.

John Macquarrie

*O Lord, baptize our hearts into a sense of the conditions
and needs of all men.*

George Fox

*O God, help us not to despise or oppose what we do not
understand.*

William Penn

*Make us worthy, Lord, to serve our fellowmen throughout
the world who live and die in poverty and hunger.
Give them, through our hands, this day their daily bread,
and by our understanding love, give peace and joy.*

Mother Teresa

O Lord, open my eyes
that I may see the need of others,
open my ears that I may hear their cries,
open my heart so that they need not be without succour.
Let me not be afraid to defend the weak
because of the anger of the strong,
nor afraid to defend the poor
because of the anger of the rich.
Show me where love and hope and faith are needed,
and use me to bring them to these places.
Open my eyes and ears that I may, this coming day,
be able to do some work of peace for thee.

Alan Paton

God, we believe that you have called us together
to broaden our experience of you and of each other.
We believe that we have been called
to help in healing the many wounds of society
and in reconciling man to man and man to God.
Help us, as individuals or together,
to work, in love, for peace, and never to lose heart.
We commit ourselves to each other –
in joy and sorrow.
We commit ourselves to all who share our belief in
*   reconciliation –*
to support and stand by them.
We commit ourselves to the way of peace –
in thought and deed.
We commit ourselves to you –
as our guide and friend.

The Corrymeela Community

Lord, we pray this day mindful of the sorry confusion of our world. Look with mercy upon this generation of your children so steeped in misery of their own contriving, so far strayed from your ways and so blinded by passions. We pray for the victims of tyranny, that they may resist oppression with courage. We pray for wicked and cruel men, whose arrogance reveals to us what the sin of our own hearts is like when it has conceived and brought forth its final fruit.

We pray for ourselves who live in peace and quietness, that we may not regard our good fortune as proof of our virtue, or rest content to have our ease at the price of other men's sorrow and tribulation.

We pray for all who have some vision of your will, despite the confusions and betrayals of human sin, that they may humbly and resolutely plan for and fashion the foundations of a just peace between men, even while they seek to preserve what is fair and just among us against the threat of malignant powers.

Reinhold Niebuhr

Divine Discontent

Hasten the time, O Lord, when no man shall live in contentment while he knows that others have need. Inspire in us and in people of all nations the desire for social justice, that the hungry may be fed, the homeless welcomed, the sick healed, and a just order established in the world, according to thy gracious will made known in Jesus Christ, our Lord.

George Appleton

We pray for the peoples of Asia *as they struggle for justice, peace and an end to wars in face of situations of desperate poverty and yet with great hopes for a new society in which human rights are carefully respected, looking for adequate ways of development, seeking to preserve their ancient and noble cultures as the context of a human existence, and as a gift to the whole human family; as Christians especially do we pray for that land sanctified by our Lord's footsteps, that it may become the crossroads of peace and fraternity.*

   Silence.

We pray for Africa *with all its richness of spirit, that its peoples may be strengthened as they build up their own nations and work for peace and justice: may they be delivered from the terrors of famine and drought, of disease, of racism, and of discouragement.*

   Silence.

We pray for the nations and peoples of Latin America, *who thirst for justice and peace, longing for fuller self-determination, striving against opression and unjust economic and social conditions and the worst kinds of poverty, yet discovering your ways of salvation in a preferential love for the poor and in the search for a just peace.*

   Silence.

We pray for Europe, *faced with the division of East and West; where the search for peace takes on a new urgency and is complicated by the arms race and the nuclear threat, by problems of injustice, by the plight of refugees, and by the selfishness of consumer societies.*

   Silence.

We pray for the peoples of the North American continent *that they may be renewed in the Christian ideals of justice and freedom, so that they may be ever more aware of their responsibilities in the family of nations and that they may give themselves to the needs of others, with respect for their aspirations and compassion for their needs, and themselves ever be just stewards of what has been entrusted to them.*

Silence.

We pray for the peoples of Oceania *in their concern to preserve their cultures and to keep their lands and their seas free from war, and as they give thanks to God for the wonders of his creation, may they be strengthened to keep true values alive and to seek, in a happy and peaceful spirit, opportunity and justice for all.*

Silence.

We pray for the United Nations Organization *and other international organizations which serve peace and understanding, that they may be strong in helping settle differences fairly, with respect for the rights of people, and without recourse to violence; we pray for political leaders who negotiate peace, that they may learn to trust each other and that the agreements they achieve may be respected. We pray for the super-powers that they may be aware of the value and responsibility of each nation in the family of nations and that they may turn from the paths that could lead to war.*

Silence.

In Prayer for Peace

6

Suffering and Hope

Peace I leave with you,
my peace I give unto you:
not as the world giveth,
give I unto you.
Let not your heart be troubled,
neither let it be afraid.

John 14.27

My Peace I Give Unto You

Blessed are the eyes that see
 The things that you have seen,
Blessed are the feet that walk
 The ways where you have been.

Blessed are the eyes that see
 The Agony of God,
Blessed are the feet that tread
 The paths his feet have trod.

Blessed are the souls that solve
 The paradox of Pain,
And find the path that, piercing it,
 Leads through to Peace again.

G. A. Studdert Kennedy

When the Jesus of the fourth Gospel proclaims to his disciples, 'Peace I leave with you; my peace I give to you, not as the world gives do I give to you' (John 14.27), the assurance most Christians tend to hear in these words is of a peace more secure and lasting than any the world can offer. But this is not precisely what is said: 'not as the world gives' suggests both that the peace in question is not of the same sort as anything we habitually call peace, and that the giving itself is of a new and different order. What is offered and the way it is offered are alike a challenge to the world's peace . . .

Illusory and corrupt forms of peace rest on a decision to ignore or repress certain dimensions of experience. But Jesus 'leaves' his peace to the apostles on the night before he suffers, before he enters into the depth of the experience of death and glory together; and when he returns as risen, marked with his crucifixion wounds, he greets the apostles with, 'Peace be with you' (John 20.19 and 21) . . .

The cross is the culmination of Jesus's living-out of peace, not just because it is a symbol of the absorbing of violence without resistance and counter-violence (though that is important enough), but because it represents the total triumph in his life of 'the Father's will' . . . For him, passing through the cross is the final peace-making. It establishes in the world of men and women the truth of an affirmation and acceptance beyond all our destructiveness, untruth and pain, telling us that we may have a 'Father' also – that we may be trustingly surrendered to the source of our life and the life of all things, and receive into our minds and hearts the stillness of Jesus's offering of himself, the peace of the cross.

Rowan Williams

Why Have You Forsaken Me?

Lord, O Lord my God
why have you forsaken me?
I am a caricature of a man
people think I am dirt
they mock me in all the papers.

I am encircled:
there are tanks all around me
machine-gunners have me in their sights:
there is barbed wire about me –
electrified wire.
I am on a list
I am called all day
they have tattooed me
and marked me with a number.
They have photographed me behind the barbed wire
all my bones can be counted
as on an X-ray film.
They have stripped me of my identity
They have led me naked to the gas–chamber
They have shared out my clothes and my shoes.

Ernesto Cardenal

Night and silence.
I listen.
Only the steps and cries of the guards,
The distant, hidden laughter of two lovers.
Do you hear nothing else, lazy sleeper?
I hear my own soul tremble and heave.
Nothing else?
I hear, I hear
The silent night thoughts
Of my fellow sufferers asleep or awake,
As if voices, cries,
As if shouts for planks to save them.
I hear the uneasy creak of the beds,
I hear chains.
I hear how sleepless men toss and turn,
Who long for freedom and deeds of wrath.
When at grey dawn sleep finds them
They murmur in dreams of their wives and children.
I hear the happy lisp of half-grown boys,
Delighting in childhood dreams;
I hear them tug at their blankets
And hide from hideous nightmares.
I hear the sighs and weak breath of the old,
Who in silence prepare for the last journey.
They have seen justice and injustice come and go;
Now they wish to see the imperishable, the eternal.
Night and silence.
Only the steps and cries of the guards.
Do you hear how in the silent house
It quakes, cracks, roars
When hundreds kindle the stirred-up flame of their
    hearts?
Their choir is silent,
But my ear is open wide:
'We the old, the young,

The sons of all tongues,
We the strong, the weak,
The sleepers, the wakeful,
We the poor, the rich,
Alike in misfortune,
The good, the bad,
Whatever we have been,
We men of many scars,
We the witnesses of those who died,
We the defiant, we the despondent,
The innocent, and the much accused,
Deeply tormented by long isolation,
Brother, we are searching, we are calling you!
Brother, do you hear me?'

Dietrich Bonhoeffer

I will live and survive

I will live and survive and be asked:
How they slammed my head against a trestle,
How I had to freeze at nights,
How my hair started to turn grey . . .
I will smile. And will crack some joke
And brush away the encroaching shadow.
And I will render homage to the dry September
That became my second birth.
And I'll be asked: 'Doesn't it hurt you to remember?'
Not being deceived by my outward flippancy.
But the former names will detonate in my memory –
Magnificent as old cannon.
And I will tell of the best people in all the earth,

The most tender, but also the most invincible,
How they said farewell, how they went to be tor-
tured,
How they waited for letters from their loved ones.
And I'll be asked: what helped us to live
When there were neither letters nor any news –
   only walls,
And the cold of the cell, and the blather of official lies,
And the sickening promises made in exchange for
   betrayal.
And I will tell of the first beauty
I saw in captivity.
A frost-covered window! No doors, nor walls,
Nor cell-bars, nor the long-endured pain –
Only a blue radiance on a tiny pane of glass,
A cast pattern – none more beautiful could be dreamt!
The more clearly you looked, the more powerfully
   dawned
Those brigand forests, campfires and birds!
And how many times there was bitter cold weather
And how many windows sparkled after that one –
But never was it repeated,
That upheaval of rainbow ice!
And anyway, what good would it be to me now,
And what would be the pretext for that festival?
Such a gift can only be received once,
And once is probably enough.

Irina Ratushinskaya

I believe in the sun even when it is not shining.
I believe in love even when feeling it not.
I believe in God even when he is silent.

Anonymous (Jewish)

O Lord,
remember not only the men and women of
good will
but also those of evil will.
But do not remember all the suffering
they have inflicted upon us;
remember the fruits we have borne
thanks to this suffering –
our comradeship, our loyalty, our humility,
our courage, our generosity,
the greatness of heart
which has grown out of all this;
and when they come to the judgement,
let all the fruits that we have borne
be their forgiveness.

Anonymous

We remember, O Lord,
those who suffer from any kind of discrimination;
thy children, and our brothers and sisters,
who are humiliated and oppressed;
we pray for those who are denied fundamental human
*   rights,*
for those who are imprisoned,
and especially those who are tortured.
Our thoughts rest a few moments with them . . .
and we pray that thy love and compassion
may sustain them always.

Week Of Prayer for World Peace

Lord, open our eyes
to the sufferings of our imprisoned brothers and sisters
so that, by our understanding and love,
we may bring them your peace and joy.
You came to set us free.
May your light shine on the captives,
relieve their suffering,
and enable us all to grow toward true freedom
in justice and harmony.

Pax Christi

Response: *Deliver them, O Lord.*
God of love and compassion.
God of freedom and justice.
From prejudice and bitterness.
From persecution and discrimination.
From the jailor and the torturer.
From condemnation and the executioner.
From despair and hopelessness.
From hatred of their enemies.
From their bondage and captivity.
From their pain and suffering.
From all evil.

Michael Evans

Response: *Lord, make us instruments of your peace.*
Lord, where there is hatred and fear and lack of peace.
Lord, where there is sorrow and sadness.
Lord, where there is persecution and oppression.
Lord, where man is made to suffer for what he believes.
Lord, where man is imprisoned because he is different.
Lord, where there is torture and pain.
Lord, where there is death for those who do no wrong.
Lord, where there are tears and despair.
Lord, where there is loneliness and hopelessness.
Lord, wherever you seem far away.

Michael Evans

Lord Jesus,
you experienced in person
torture and death
as a prisoner of conscience.
You were beaten and flogged,
and sentenced to an agonizing death
though you had done no wrong.
Be now with prisoners of conscience
throughout the world.
Be with them in their fear and loneliness,
in the agony of physical and mental torture,
and in the face of execution and death.
Stretch out your hands in power
to break their chains.
Be merciful to the oppressor and the torturer,
and place a new heart within them.
Forgive all injustice in our lives,
and transform us to be
instruments of your peace,
for by your wounds we are healed.

Amnesty International

7

The Peace of God

What ails my soul, that maketh long complaint
to men, but for the fear of God is faint?
Its very plaint forbiddeth its release,
augments its terror, and destroys its peace.
Would it but come with humble love sincere
unto its Master, he would draw it near;
but since it chooseth who his creatures are
above their Fashioner, he keeps it far,
and makes its need yet more: but let it flee
to him, he'll grant it fully satiety.
Unto his creatures it complains, as though
they have the power to work it weal or woe:
but would it lay all matters at his feet
in true sincerity and trust complete,
He would not leave it in its long despairs,
but give it gladness in return for cares . . .

How well by God assisted is that soul
which, seeking refuge, gains in God its goal!
Rank and renown it winneth from its King,
and at the founts of faith finds watering:
it soars to God in loveliness of thought,
by God with love and kindness it is sought,
and if in need unto the Lord it cries
He hears its prayer, and speedily supplies.
He gives it patience in calamity,
and to its call his hand is ever free.

Abu Hamid al-Ghazali (attributed)

[85]

Buddha said: There are four meditations:

The first meditation is the meditation of love, in which you must so adjust your heart, that you long for the weal and welfare of all beings, including the happiness of your enemies.

The second meditation is the meditation of compassion, in which you think of all beings in distress, vividly representing in your imagination their sorrows and anxieties so as to arouse a deep compassion for them in your soul.

The third meditation is the meditation of joy, in which you think of the prosperity of others and rejoice at their rejoicings.

The fourth meditation is the meditation on serenity, in which you rise above love and hate, tyranny and oppression, wealth and want, and regard your own fate with impartial calmness and perfect tranquillity.

The Brahma Vihara

God, you have given us the treasure of peace,
an experience greater than all worldly treasures.
We must learn the lesson of peace.
I the soul am peaceful.
God our Father is the ocean of peace.
If we experience peace from the ocean of peace,
just for a few moments,
this becomes a blessing for a lifetime.
Through the blessing of peace,
the seed of war and conflict finishes.
The seed is anger.
If this seed is destroyed
then peace will be achieved in the world.
Our hearts give thanks to the ocean of peace
for the treasure and blessing of peace.

Anonymous (Hindu)

Great is thy glory, for great is thy name.
Great is thy glory, for thy justice is true.
Great is thy glory, for eternal is the seat.
Great is thy glory, for thou divinest our inner thoughts.

Great is thy glory, for thou givest unasked,
Great is thy glory, for thou art all-in-all.
The Lord is the giver;
The Lord is the haven of peace;
The peace that reigns on snow-clad mountains.

Anonymous (Sikh)

My life of the spirit is impoverished
when I neglect communing with thee.
A tense silence holds between me and thee
when I cease to meet thee and confer with thee.
My spiritual vision is blurred.
I cannot feel thy presence,
I cannot see thy radiant face . . .
Like a land bird that finds no solid object to alight upon,
when it is out to sea,
I am lost when I leave thee
and find no place of safety for my misguided soul.
My life is wrapped up in thee and in thy protecting love.
Hold me by my hands and guide me
and I will follow thee wherever thou dost lead me.
I will serve thee to the end of my life,
till thou dost call me back from my earthly sojourn
to my final rest and repose in thee.

M. N. Dhalla

May we not worry but believe in thee, our Great Parent.

Bunjiro

Blessed art thou, O Lord our God, King of the universe, who makest the bands of sleep to fall upon mine eyes, and slumber upon mine eyelids. May it be thy will, O Lord my God and God of my fathers, to suffer me to lie down in peace and to let me rise up again in peace. Let not my thoughts trouble me, nor evil dreams, nor evil fancies, but let my rest be perfect before thee . . . Blessed art thou, O Lord, who givest light to the whole world in thy glory.

The Hebrew Prayer Book

Let there be love and understanding among us; let peace and friendship be our shelter from life's storms. Eternal God, help us to walk with good companions, to live with hope in our hearts and eternity in our thoughts, that we may lie down in peace and rise up to find our hearts waiting to do your will.

Anonymous (Jewish)

O God, I make my complaint unto thee,
out of my feebleness and the vanity of my wishes.
I am insignificant in the sight of men,
O thou most merciful!
God of the weak!
Thou art my God!
Forsake me not.
Leave me not a prey to strangers nor to my enemies.
If thou art not offended, I am safe.
I seek refuge in the light of thy countenance,
by which all darkness is dispelled
and peace cometh in the here and the hereafter.

Anonymous (Muslim)

O my God, my soul is a ship adrift in seas of her own
will, where there is no shelter from thee save in thee.
Appoint for her, O God, in the name of God, her
course and its harbour.

Anonymous (Muslim)

Grant me, O God, to seek thy satisfaction with my
satisfaction and the delight of a father in his child,
remembering thee in my love for thee with serene
tranquillity and firm resolve.

Anonymous (Muslim)

Can any praise be worthy of the Lord's majesty?
How magnificent his strength!
How inscrutable his wisdom!
Man is one of your creatures, Lord,
and his instinct is to praise you . . .
The thought of you stirs him so deeply
that he cannot be content
unless he praises you,
because you made us for yourself
and our hearts find no peace
until they rest in you.

St Augustine of Hippo

Lo, fainter now lie spread the shades of night,
   and upward spread the trembling gleams of morn,
suppliant we bend before the Lord of Light,
   and pray at early dawn,
that this sweet charity may all our sin
   forgive, and make our miseries to cease;
may grant us health, grant us the gift divine
   of everlasting peace.
Father Supreme, this grace on us confer;
   and thou, O Son by an eternal birth!
with thee, coequal Spirit, comforter!
   whose glory fills the earth.

St Gregory the Great

Dear Lord and Father of mankind,
Forgive our foolish ways!
Re-clothe us in our rightful mind,
In purer lives thy service find,
In deeper reverence praise.

Drop thy still dews of quietness,
Till all our strivings cease;
Take from our souls the strain and stress,
And let our ordered lives confess
The beauty of thy peace.

John Greenleaf Whittier

O God of peace, who hast taught us that in returning and
rest we shall be saved, in quietness and in confidence shall
be our strength: by the might of thy Spirit lift us, we pray
thee, to thy presence where we may be still and know that
thou art God.

Anonymous (Christian)

The Lord bless thee, and keep thee:
The Lord make his face shine upon thee, and be gracious
*   unto thee:*
The Lord lift up his countenance upon thee, and give thee
*   peace.*

Numbers 6.24–7

Peace be on you, and the mercy of God and his blessings.

Muslim greeting

May all beings be happy and at their ease,
Free from pain, fear, distress or enmity;
Untroubled, well, unharmed, in peace.

Buddhist blessing

Deep peace of the Running Wave to you.
Deep peace of the Flowing Air to you.
Deep peace of the Quiet Earth to you.
Deep peace of the Shining Stars to you.
Deep peace of the Son of Peace to you.

Celtic Benediction

The Way of Empathy

Hinduism
This is the sum of all true rightousness: do nothing to your neighbour which you would not have him do to you after.

Zoroastrianism
That nature only is good when it shall not do to another whatever is not good for its own self.

Jainism
A man of religion should treat all beings as he himself would be treated.

Buddhism
Hurt not others in ways that you yourself would find hurtful.

Confucianism
Surely it is a maxim of loving-kindness: do not to others that which you would not have them do to you.

Taoism
Regard your neighbour's gain as your own gain, and your neighbour's loss as your own loss.

Judaism
What is hateful to you, do not to your fellow men. That is the entire Law; all the rest is commentary.

Christianity
Whatever you wish that men would do to you, do so to them; for this is the law and the prophets.

Islam
No one of you is a believer until he desires for his brother that which he desires for himself.

Sikhism
As you deem yourself, so deem others. Then you shall become a partner in heaven.

Baha'i
Regard not that which benefits yourself, but hold on that which benefits mankind.

The peace of God,

which passeth all understanding,

keep your hearts and minds

in the knowledge and love of God,

and of his Son Jesus Christ our Lord:

And the blessing of God Almighty,

the Father, the Son,

and the Holy Spirit,

be amongst you

and remain with you always.

Amen.

PUBLISHER'S NOTES ON SOURCES

x **Satish Kumar** (1936–). Member of the Jain community who, with Mother Teresa, launched this prayer in London in August 1981. Since then people of all religions have used the prayer in peace meetings throughout the world. The words, which are an adapatation of a passage in the Hindu Upanishads, have been translated into over forty languages.
—The Prayer for Peace (Seniors Farm House, Shaftesbury, Dorset).

1 Conflict and Division

3 **Jeremiah 8.11** (7th cent. BC).
Isaiah 57.15–21 (6th cent. BC).
—Both from the Authorized (King James) Version, 1611.
4 **The Qur'an.** Sacred book of Islam, revealed to the prophet Muhammad c, AD610–630.
—Surah 100. 1–10. Translated by Kenneth Cragg.
Lao Tzu (6th cent. BC?). Reputed founder of Taoism. From the *Tao Te Ching* ('The Way and its Power'), one of the most important of China's religious writings.
—*Peace on Earth* (UNESCO, Paris, 1980).
Zarathustra (6th cent. BC?) Iranian prophet and founder of Zoroastrianism. 'The Wise Lord' is a translation of 'Ahura Mazda', the name for God in the Zoroastrian scriptures, the Avesta.
—B. S. Surti, ed., *Thus Spake Zarathustra* (Ramakrishna Vedanta Centre, 2nd edn 1981).
5 **Martin Luther King, Jr** (Chr. 1929–68). Black American clergyman and civil rights leader who advocated non-violent civil disobedience. Winner of the 1964 Nobel Peace Prize, he was assassinated four years later.
—James M. Washington, ed., *A Testament of Hope: The Essential Writings of Martin Luther King, Jr* (Harper and Row 1986).
6 **Cecil Day Lewis** (Chr. 1904–72). Born in Ireland, he became poet laureate in 1968. A member of the Communist party during the mid-thirties, his earlier poetry reflects his social and political commitments, while his later poems are more personal.
—C. Day Lewis, *Collected Poems* (Jonathan Cape 1954).

7 **Kenneth Cragg** (Chr. 1913–). Distinguished British scholar of comparative religion and a world authority on Islam.

8 **Thomas Merton** (Chr. 1915–68). Born in France, a Trappist monk who became America's leading spiritual writer this century. He was a champion of non-violence at home and of peace among nations. He also became a student of Eastern mysticism, developing a special interest in Zen Buddhism.
  —Thomas Merton, *On Peace* (Mowbray 1976).

9 **Pope John Paul II** (Chr. 1920–). Born in Poland, Karol Wojtyla became Pope in October 1978. World peace is one of his most passionate concerns, as evidenced by his invitation to the world's religious leaders to join him in a day of prayer for peace, held in Assisi in October 1986. This particular prayer was spoken by Pope John Paul during his visit to Hiroshima in 1981.

10 **Pax Christi**. Founded in 1946, an international Catholic peace movement which also welcomes members from other denominations. It seeks to promote justice and reconciliation (especially in Northern Ireland), better international relations, disarmament, peace education, and the development of a spirituality of non-violence.
  Week of Prayer for World Peace. Based in London, a multifaith movement which was founded in 1974 by an informal group under the chairmanship of Dr Edward Carpenter. Every year since then many thousands of individuals, as well as many local groups of believers around the world, have joined in the prayers for each day of the Week, which is always chosen to include United Nations Day (24 October).
  —From the prayer leaflet for 1982.

11 **Baptist Peace Fellowship**.
  —From a service for Remembrance Sunday.

12 **Nahman of Bratslav** (Jew. 1772–1819). Hasidic leader and mystic. Modern Hasidic mysticism originated in Podolia towards the mid-eighteenth century, inspired by Rabbi Israel b. Eliezer (1700–60).
  —Alan Unterman, *The Wisdom of the Jewish Mystics* (Sheldon Press 1976).
  Dalai Lama (Bud. 1935–). Traditional religious and political leader of Tibet until its occupation by China in 1959. Exiled from his home country, the present Dalai Lama works to preserve the religious and cultural heritage of Tibet from his centre in Dharamsala, N.W. India.
  Karma (lit. 'action, deed, work'): a Sanskrit word denoting not only a person's acts but also their physical or ethical consequences. In Buddhism, Hinduism and Jainism the word is

linked to the doctrine of transmigration, according to which good *karma* brings a good afterlife and evil *karma* brings an afterlife of trial and suffering.

2 *Visions of Unity*

15 **Micah 4.1–5**. (8th–7th cent. BC). From the Authorized (King James) Version, 1611. Part of the third verse forms the motto of the United Nations Organization.

16 **Robert Runcie** (Chr. 1921–). Archbishop of Canterbury (1980–). From the sermon given at the Falkland Islands service, St Paul's Cathedral, July 1982.
—Robert Runcie, *Windows onto God* (SPCK 1983).

17 **Islamic Council of Europe**. Founded in 1973 and based in London, it aims to promote good relations between the Islamic world and the West.

18 **Sarvepalli Radhakrishnan** (Hin. 1888–1975). Former President of India (1962–7). A leading exponent of Hindu philosophy, he advocated balance between action and contemplation and pleaded for close co-operation between the world's religions.
—Sarvepalli Radhakrishnan, *The Hindu View of Life* (Allen & Unwin 1927).

19 **Walpola Rahula** (Bud. 1907–). Renowned Buddhist scholar and monk from Sri Lanka.
—Walpola Rahula, *What the Buddha Taught* (Gordon Fraser, 2nd edn 1967).
Nirvana (lit. 'blowing out, extinguishing'): a Sanskrit word used in Buddhism to denote the indescribable state of peace and enlightenment achieved by liberated beings after death.

20 **Bahá'u'lláh** (1817–92). Iranian mystic and founder of the Baha'i faith. From their present headquarters in Haifa, Israel, the Baha'i teach that all religions are expressions of a continuous and harmonious revelation, and that all of mankind should work for universal peace.
—Bahá'u'lláh, *Tablets of Bahá'u'lláh revealed after the Kitáb-i-Aqdas* (Baha'i World Centre, Haifa, 1978).
UNESCO. Founded in 1946, its primary aim is to contribute to peace and security in the world by promoting collaboration among nations through education, science, culture and communication.
—From the UNESCO constitution, prepared by a conference convened in London in 1945.

21 ***Forms of Prayer for Jewish Worship**: Daily, Sabbath and Occasional Prayers* (Reform Synagogues of Great Britain, 7th edn 1977).

Liberal Jewish Prayer book (The Liberal Jewish Synagogue 1923).

22–3 **William Temple** (Chr. 1881–1944). Former Archbishop of Canterbury (1942–4). During the world war of 1939–45 he worked with other British church leaders on a statement of principles which would provide a just basis for a post-war settlement.
—William Temple, ed., *A Manual of Prayers for Wartime* (Mowbray 1939).

24 **George Appleton** (Chr. 1902–). Former Archbishop of Jerusalem (1969–74), where he worked to promote reconciliation between Israelis and Palestinians. He remains active in the cause of peace and understanding between people of different faiths.
—George Appleton, *Jerusalem Prayers for the World Today* (SPCK 1974).

25 **James Martineau** (1805–1900). British Unitarian philosopher and pastor.
—*Orders of Worship for use in Unitarian and Free Christian Congregations* (Lindsey Press 1932).
Anonymous (Muslim). Source unknown.

26 **The Vedas**. The most ancient and sacred scriptures of the Hindu faith, probably composed c. 1500–800BC.
—Solomans, ed., *Prayers for the Future of Mankind* (Wolfe Publishing 1975).
—W. Owen Cole, *Six Religions in the Twentieth Century* (Hulton Educational 1984).

27, 28 **Anonymous (Hindu)**. Both written by a Raja Yoga student at the Brahma Kumaris World Spiritual University, London.

29 **Thich Nhat Hanh** (Bud 1916–) Vietnamese scholar, monk, poet and contemplative nominated by Martin Luther King, Jr for the Nobel Peace Prize in recognition of his work for reconciliation in Vietnam. This quotation is from a litany used by the Venerable Thich Nhat Hanh at an interfaith gathering in Canterbury in 1976.
—George Appleton, ed., *The Oxford Book of Prayer* (OUP 1985).

30 **Zarathustra**. See note 4.
Guru Gobind Singh (1666–1708). Last of the ten gurus who succeeded Nanak (1469–1539), the founder of Sikhism. The Sikhs believe in one God who dwells everywhere and is accessible to all mankind.

31 **Anonymous (African Traditional)**. From a prayer of the Ewe people, found in Benin, Ghana and Togo.
—A. M. di Nola, ed., *The Prayers of Man* (Heinemann 1962).

'Abdu'l-Bahá (1844–1920). Eldest son of Bahá'u'lláh, whom he succeeded as head of the Baha'i community. See note 20.

3 The Way of Love

35 **The Dhammapada**. A collection of sayings attributed to Gautama Buddha (c.560–480BC), forming the most famous book of the Pali Canon. It covers almost every aspect of Buddhist teaching, and has had immense influence in the Buddhist world for over two millennia.

—Jack Austin, trans., *The Dhammapada* (The Buddhist Society, 3rd edn 1983).

The Metta Sutta. *Metta* is the Pali word for loving kindness. These famous lines from the short *sutta* (thread of teaching) devoted to *metta* are found among the discourses attributed to the Buddha which appear in the Sutta Pitaka of the Pali Canon.

—Walpola Rahula, *What the Buddha Taught* (Gordon Fraser, 2nd edn 1967).

36 **Thich Nhat Hanh**. See note 29.

37 **Mahatma Gandhi** (Hin. 1869–1948). Indian religious leader, moral teacher and social reformer. He opposed discrimination against Indians in South Africa (1893–1914) and then returned to India to lead his country to independence. He was assassinated the year after independence had been achieved. See also note 49.

—Peter D. Smith, ed., *Peace Offerings* (Stainer & Bell 1986).

Ahimsa (lit. 'non-killing'): a Sanskrit word used in Eastern religions to denote the doctrine of not harming or wishing to harm any living creature.

38 **Swami Ramdas** (1884–1963). Renowned Indian spiritual thinker who advocated a continuous remembrance of God and the practice of a Universal Religion of Love and Service.

—*Thus Speaks Ramdas* (Ramakrishna Vedanta Centre, 9th edn 1984).

Swami Vivekananda (Hin. 1863–1902). Eminent Indian philosopher who became chief disciple of the Hindu saint, Sri Ramakrishna (1834–86). He founded the Ramakrishna Mission, and advocated closer interaction between Eastern and Western religions.

—*Thus Spake Vivekananda* (Ramakrishna Vedanta Centre, 14th edn 1980).

39 **Abraham Isaac Kook** (Jew. 1865–1935). Born in Latvia, a Jewish scholar and mystic who became the first Chief Rabbi of Palestine (1921–35).

—Abraham Isaac Kook (trans. Ben Zion Bokser), *The Lights of Penitence, Lights of Holiness, etc.* (SPCK 1979).

Martin Buber (Jew. 1878–1965). Born in Austria, a Jewish philosopher who became a leading exponent of Hasidic mysticism.

—Martin Buber, *I and Thou* (T. & T. Clark).

40 **Luke 6.27–35** (1st cent. AD). Words of Jesus from the 'Sermon on the Plain', which parallels the Gospel of Matthew's 'Sermon on the Mount' (5.38–48).

1 Corinthians 13.4–8 (mid 1st cent. AD). Words of St Paul, written to commend the way of harmony to the Christian Church.

—Both from the Revised Standard Version, 2nd edn 1971.

41 **Leonard Wilson** (Chr. 1897–1970). Former Bishop of Singapore (1941–3) who was imprisoned and tortured by the Japanese during the Second World War. He was later appointed Bishop of Birmingham (1953–69).

—Roy McKay, *John Leonard Wilson: Confessor for the Faith* (Hodder and Stoughton 1973).

Desmond Tutu (Chr. 1931–). Archbishop of Capetown (1986–). A black theologian and leading opponent of South Africa's apartheid régime, he was awarded the 1984 Nobel Peace Prize.

—Desmond Tutu, *Hope and Suffering: Sermons and Speeches* (Fount 1984).

42 **The Vedas**. See note 26.

Swami Yatiswarananda, ed./trans., *Universal Prayers* (Ramakrishna Vedanta Centre 1977).

Anonymous (Hindu). See note 27.

43 **Anonymous (American Indian)**. From a prayer recited on the World Day of Prayer for Peace in Assisi in October 1986.

The Talmud. Sacred collection of Jewish oral law and traditions, composed c. 200BC–AD500.

—*A Rabbinic Anthology* (Macmillan).

Anonymous (Jewish). Source unknown.

44 **Anonymous (Christian)**. From a Syrian Catholic Service of Mutual Forgiveness on Holy Saturday.

—*Prayer with the Harp of the Spirit: the Prayer of Asian Churches* (Vagamon, Kerala, India, 1985).

Anonymous (Christian). A prayer dating from 1913, later used in Rome to address the Sacred Heart of Jesus. Very soon it was seen to express the spirit and ideals of St Francis of Assisi and began to be called his prayer. St Francis (Chr. c. 1182–1226) founded the Order of Friars Minor, the first of a family of Franciscan Orders, a movement marked by humility and solidarity with the poor. He strove to bring peace in Europe and between Christians and Muslims.

45 **Thomas à Kempis** (Chr. c.1380–1471). Born in Germany, a

monastic writer who spent most of his life in the Netherlands. He is credited with the composition of the spiritual classic *The Imitation of Christ*.

—Barbara Greene and Victor Gollancz, *God of a Hundred Names* (Gollancz 1962).

The Book of Common Prayer. First published in 1549, the 1662 version of the BCP was until recently the sole official service book of the Church of England. This collect is for Quinquagesima, the Sunday before Lent.

46 **Thomas Merton**. See note 8.

—Thomas Merton, *The Asian Journal* (Lawrence Pollinger).

4 The Way of Truth

49 **Mahatma Gandhi**. See note 37. Truth (*satya*) was a key concept in Gandhi's religious and political thought. Combined with non-violence (*ahimsa*) and self-sacrifice (*tapas*), it formed the basis of the political method which he called *satyagraha* (lit. 'truth-force').

—Thomas Merton, *Conjectures of a Guilty Bystander* (Sheldon Press 1977).

Sangharakshita (Bud. 1925–). An English-born scholar and monk who founded the Western Buddhist Order, which represents an eclectic form of Buddhism intended to aid the transplantation and adaptation of Buddhism in the West.

—Sangharakshita, *Buddhism, World Peace and Nuclear War* (Windhorse Publications 1984).

50 **Dag Hammarksjöld** (Chr. 1905–61). Born in Sweden, he became Secretary-General of the UN in 1953 and did much to extend its influence for peace. He was killed in a plane crash while trying to mediate a reconciliation between warring factions in the Congo. Posthumous winner of the 1961 Nobel Peace Prize.

—Dag Hammarksjöld, *Markings* (Faber 1964).

51 **Alexander Solzhenitsyn** (Chr. 1918–). Russian novelist and winner of the 1970 Nobel Prize for Literature. His criticisms of the dehumanizing effects of Stalinism led to his nine-year imprisonment in 1945. He now lives in Switzerland, having been exiled in 1974 for actions allegedly incompatible with Soviet citizenship.

—Alexander Solzhenitsyn (trans. Nicholas Bethell), *Nobel Prize Lecture* (Stenvalley Press 1973).

St Maximilian Kolbe (Chr. 1894–1941). A Polish Franciscan priest who gave his life for a fellow prisoner in Auschwitz. He was canonized in 1982.

—Mary Craig, *Candles in the Dark* (Hodder and Stoughton 1984).

52 **Jerzy Popieluszko** (Chr. 1947–1984). Polish priest whose support for the outlawed trade union Solidarity led to his abduction and murder by members of the Polish Secret Police.
—From a sermon delivered at the Mass for the country, December 1983. Translated by Grazyna Sikorska of Keston College, Kent. Pope John Paul II's Message for the World Day of Peace 1980 is loosely quoted; the accurate text is in *Ways of Peace* (Vatican Press 1986), pp. 136–46.

53 **Anonymous (Buddhist)**. Written by a member of the Chithurst Buddhist Monastery, England, and recited at the ceremonial inauguration of the London Peace Pagoda in May 1985. The pagoda, which is situated in Battersea Park, was built by members of the Japanese Buddhist Order Nipponzan Myohoji, in association with the Greater London Council, and at the request of the Order's Founder and Preceptor, the Most Venerable Nichidatsu Fujii (1884–1985).
Anonymous (Zoroastrian). From the Yasna, a liturgical book which is found in the Zoroastrian scriptures, the Avesta.
—Muller, *Sacred Books of the East* (Clarendon Press).

54 **Anonymous (Jain)**. From the Contemplation in the Shire Digambar Jain Temple in celebration of the Silver Jubilee of the Missionaries of Charity (founded by Mother Teresa of Calcutta in October 1950).
—Mother Teresa (ed. Kathryn Spink), *In the Silence of the Heart* (SPCK 1983).

55 **Anonymous (Muslim)**. From a selection of 'prayers for this world and the hereafter', translated by M. Abdul Hamid Siddiqui.
Rabbi Lionel Blue (Jew. 1930–   ). One of the most popular religious writers and broadcasters in Britain, he has done much to promote good will and understanding between the Jewish and Christian faiths.
—From a 'prayer for international understanding' in *Forms of Prayer for Jewish Worship: Daily, Sabbath and Occasional Prayers* (Reform Synagogues of Great Britain, 7th edn 1977).

5 *Justice and Reconciliation*

59 **Mo Tzu** (5th cent. BC?). Chinese religious and ethical teacher, whose followers rivalled the Confucians. He advocated universal benevolence and was opposed to offensive warfare.
—Geoffrey Parrinder, ed., *Themes for Living*, vol. 3 (Hulton Educational).

The Qur'an. See note 4.

—Surah 2.153. Translated by Imaduddin Ahmed Sheikh.

Bahá'u'lláh. See note 20.

—The Baha'i Publishing Trust, Leicester, England.

60 **Matthew 5.3–10** (1st cent.AD). The first eight 'beatitudes', with which Jesus began the Sermon on the Mount.

—From the Revised Standard Version, 2nd edn 1971.

61 **Oscar Romero** (Chr. 1917–80). Appointed Archbishop of San Salvador in 1977, he opposed the rampant injustice and oppression in El Salvador and was assassinated three years later.

—Archbishop Romero (ed. Jon Sobrino, trans. M. Walsh), *Romero, Martyr for Liberation: The Last Two Homilies of Archbishop Romero* (CIIR 1982).

Helder Câmara (Chr. 1909–). Former Catholic Archbishop of Olinda and Reçife in N.E. Brazil (1964–85). He has played a leading part in the movement for non-violent social reform in his own country, and has been influential in calling the Church's attention to the plight of the poor throughout Latin America. Awarded the 1970 Martin Luther King Jr International Peace Prize, he has twice been nominated for the Nobel Peace Prize.

—Dom Helder Câmara (trans. D. Livingstone), *The Desert is Fertile* (Sheed and Ward 1976).

62 **Basil Hume** (Chr. 1923–). Cardinal Archbishop of Westminster (1976–), President of the Council of European Bishops' Conferences (1978–87) and former Abbot of Ampleforth.

—From his address to the European Laity Forum in Dublin in July 1984.

63 **Allan Boesak** (Chr. 1946–). South African theologian, a leading opponent of apartheid and President of the World Alliance of Reformed Churches (1982–)

—Allan Boesak, *Black and Reformed: Apartheid, Liberation and the Calvinist Tradition* (Orbis, New York, 1984).

64–5 **John Macquarrie** (Chr. 1919–). Former Lady Margaret Professor of Divinity, and Canon of Christ Church, Oxford (1970–86).

—John Macquarrie, *The Concept of Peace* (SCM 1973).

66 **George Fox** (Chr. 1624–91). English religious writer and preacher who founded the Society of Friends (Quakers). Friends believe that the divine light of Christ is present in people of all nations, and have been a major influence for peace, the relief of suffering and social reform.

William Penn (Chr. 1644–1718). English Quaker, founder of Pennsylvania, and important influence in the development of religious toleration in the West.

Mother Teresa (Chr. 1910–). Born in Yugoslavia, of Albanian parents, a Roman Catholic nun who has devoted herself to the relief of the suffering in the slums of Calcutta. She founded the Missionaries of Charity (Sisters) in 1950, and the Missionary Brothers of Charity in 1963. The International Co-workers of Mother Teresa, founded in 1968, provide free service to the poor and destitute, irrespective of caste, creed or nationality. Mother Teresa has received numerous awards, including the 1979 Nobel Peace Prize.

67 **Alan Paton** (Chr. 1903–). Born in Natal, he became President of the new Liberal Party of South Africa in 1953, outlawed by the Pretoria government in 1968. He is the author of several important novels and short stories.
—Alan Paton, *Instrument of Thy Peace* (Fount, 2nd edn 1983).
The Corrymeela Community. Based in Belfast, a fellowship of Christians from all of the main Christian traditions in Northern Ireland. Founded in 1965, it is committed to witness and pray for peace in Ireland and throughout the world.

68 **Reinhold Niebuhr** (Chr. 1892–1971). America's leading Protestant theologian and ethicist this century. His advocacy of Christian realism, which involved a forceful restatement of mankind's original sin, had a widespread influence on the social and political institutions of his country.
—Richard Harries, ed., *Praying Round the Clock* (Mowbray 1982).
George Appleton. See note 24.
—George Appleton, *One Man's Prayers* (SPCK, 2nd edn 1977).

69–70 *In Prayer for Peace*. Extracts from the invitations to prayer recited by representatives of the Christian Churches and Communions on the World Day of Prayer for Peace held in Assisi in October 1986.

6 *Suffering and Hope*

73 **John 14.27** (Chr. 1st cent. AD). From one of Christ's final discourses to his disciples before his trial and crucifixion.
G. A. Studdert Kennedy (Chr. 1883–1929). Of Irish descent, an Anglican priest and poet who was a much-loved chaplain to the forces during the First World War.
—*The Rhymes of G. A. Studdert Kennedy* (Hodder and Stoughton 1940).

74 **Rowan Williams** (Chr. 1950–). Lady Margaret Professor of Divinity, and Canon of Christ Church, Oxford (1986–).
—Rowan Williams, *The Truce of God* (Fount 1983).

75 **Ernesto Cardenal** (Chr. 1925–). Born in Nicaragua, a

Roman Catholic priest, poet and mystic who helped to inspire the political revolution which led to the overthrow of the Somoza dictatorship in July 1979. He was appointed Minister of Culture in the new government. His poetry, of which this adaptation of Psalm 21 (22) is an example, has been translated into every major language.

—Ernesto Cardenal, *Psalms* (Sheed and Ward 1981).

76 **Dietrich Bonhoeffer** (Chr. 1906–45). German Lutheran pastor, theologian and martyr. He worked with Martin Niem-öller to oppose the 'German Christians' who were sponsored by the Nazis. His involvement in a plot to assassinate Hitler led to his execution by the Gestapo.

—Dietriech Bonhoeffer (ed. Eberhard Bethge, trans. R. H. Fuller), *Letters and Papers from Prison* (SCM 1953). These lines are from the long poem called 'Night Voices in Tegel'.

77 **Irina Ratushinskaya** (Chr. 1954–). Russian poet and human rights protester. In March 1983 she was sentenced to seven years in a 'strict régime' concentration camp, followed by five years of internal exile. Her repeated hunger strikes resulted in increasingly harsh treatment, including long periods of solitary confinement in an unheated punishment cell. Severe ill-health, combined with intense international pressure on the Soviet authorites, led to her unconditional release in October 1986.

—Irina Ratushinskaya (trans. David McDuff), *No, I'm Not Afraid* (Bloodaxe Books 1986).

79 **Anonymous** These lines were found on the wall of a house in which victims of Nazi persecution had hidden during the Second World War.
Anonymous. Written by an unknown prisoner in Ravensbrück concentration camp, this prayer was found on a piece of wrapping paper near the body of a dead child.

80 **Week of Prayer for World Peace**. See note 10.
—From the prayer leaflet for 1974.
Pax Christi. See note 10.

81 **Michael Evans** (Chr. 1951–). Roman Catholic priest and Chairman of the Religious Bodies Liaison Panel of Amnesty International, British Section (1984–).
—Michael Evans, ed., *Let My People Go! A source-book of prayer for prisoners of conscience* (Kevin Mayhew 1979).

82 **Amnesty International**. Founded in 1961, a worldwide human rights organization which works impartially for the release of prisoners of conscience, provided they have neither used nor advocated violence. It opposes torture and capital punishment, and advocates prompt and fair trials for all political prisoners. Winners of the 1977 Nobel Peace Prize.

—From a prayer card used by Amnesty International's Religious Bodies Liaison Panel.

7   The Peace of God

85 **Abu Hamid Al-Ghazali** (Mus. 1058–1111). Born in Iran, a Sufi poet and mystic widely regarded as the greatest theologian and philosopher of Islam.
—A. J. Arberry, trans., '*A Poem of the Soul*' (attributed to Al-Ghazali), *The Muslim World*, vol. 30 (1940).

86 **The Brahma Vihara**. In Buddhism, these four methods of meditation are intended to achieve four sublime states of life or mind (lit. 'divine dwelling-places').
—Swami Suddhasatwananda, *Thus Spake the Buddha* (Ramakrishna Vedanta Centre 1983).

87 **Julian of Norwich** (Chr. c. 1342–1420). English mystic whose *Revelations of Divine Love* has become one of the most popular of spiritual classics. Her theology emphasizes the primacy of God's love, expressed in the redemptive work of Christ, which promises salvation and peace for all creation.
—Julian of Norwich (trans. C. Wolters), *Revelations of Divine Love* (Penguin 1966).

88 **Anthony Bloom** (Chr. 1914–   ). Metropolitan of the Russian Orthodox Patriarchal Church in Great Britain and Ireland (diocese of Sourozh). Born in Switzerland, he has written mainly on the meaning and practice of prayer.
—Metropolitan Anthony and Georges Lefebvre, *Courage to Pray* (DLT 1984).

89 **Sheila Cassidy** (Chr. 1937–   ). Roman Catholic doctor and writer. She left England in 1971 to work in Chile, where she suffered imprisonment and torture as a result of treating a wounded guerrilla.
—Sheila Cassidy, *Prayer for Pilgrims* (Fount 1980).

90 **Rabindranath Tagore** (Hin. 1861–1941). Indian poet, novelist and dramatist who became the first Asian to win the Nobel Prize for Literature. He did much to encourage the growth of India's national awareness, while his spirituality remains universal in its appeal.
—Rabindranath Tagore, *Collected Poems and Plays* (Macmillan 1916).

91 **Anonymous (Hindu)**. See note 27.
Anonymous (Sikh). From the Adi Granth, the scriptures of the Sikh religion, largely composed by Guru Arjan (1563–1606), the fifth of the ten Sikh gurus.

92 **M. N. Dhalla** (1875–1956). Born into a Parsi priestly family, he became high priest of the Karachi Zoroastrians and a major

influence throughout the modern Parsi community. The Parsi faith is essentially Zoroastrian, combined with some Indian teachings and customs.

—M. N. Dhalla, *Homage unto Ahura Mazda* (B. T. Anklesaria, Dhalla Memorial Inst., Karachi, 1970).

Bunjiro Kawate (1814–83). Japanese Shintoist and founder of the Konko-Kyo sect.

93 **The Hebrew Prayer Book**. From 'Prayers before retiring to rest at night'.

—*The Authorized Daily Prayer Book of the United Hebrew Congregations of the British Commonwealth of Nations* (Eyre and Spottiswoode, 2nd edn 1962).

Anonymous (Jewish). Source unknown.

94 **Anonymous (Muslim)**.

—M. L. El-Diwany; *Reflections* (The Muslim College, London).

Anonymous (Muslim). From two Sufi prayers, translated by Kenneth Cragg. Sufi mysticism emerged in the early days of Islam, reaching the peak of its popularity and influence between the 16th and 18th centuries.

—Kenneth Cragg, *The Wisdom of the Sufis* (Sheldon Press 1976).

95 **St Augustine of Hippo** (Chr. 354–430). Born in North Africa, he became Bishop of Hippo Regius from c.396. He is one of the most influential theologians in the entire history of the Western Church

—Saint Augustine (trans. R. S. Pine-Coffin), *Confessions* (Penguin 1961).

St Gregory the Great (Chr. c.540–604). The last great Latin Father, he became Pope in 590. Among the many achievements of his pontificate was the conversion of England in c.597 under St Augustine of Canterbury (d. c.605). This 'morning hymn' by St Gregory has been specially suggested for this anthology by the present Pope, His Holiness John Paul II.

96 **John Greenleaf Whittier** (Chr. 1807–92). American Quaker poet who played an important part in the Anti-Slavery Movement. He wrote several well-known hymns, including 'Dear Lord and Father of mankind', from which these two verses are taken.

—*The English Hymnal* (OUP and Mowbray, 2nd edn 1933).

Anonymous (Christian). The writer of this prayer had in mind the words of Isaiah 30.15 and Psalm 46.10.

97 **Numbers 6.24–7** (c.6th cent. BC?). This traditional priestly blessing is probably of far greater antiquity than the book of Numbers in which it is now found. It has continued to be used in temple, synagogue and church.

—From the Authorized (King James) Version, 1611.

Muslim greeting. In Islam the peace-greeting is known as the *salam* (the Arabic word for peace, related to the Hebrew word *shalom*). The expression 'peace be upon you' occurs in the Qur'an (Surah 6.54) and has remained the basic form of greeting among Muslims to this day.

Buddhist blessing. This version of a traditional Buddhist blessing was translated by Edward Conze, formerly Professor of Indian Studies, University of Washington, Seattle.

Celtic Benediction. These lines exemplify the awareness of God's pervasive presence in all creation, which is characteristic of Celtic Christianity.

—*Iona Community Worship Book* (Wild Goose Publications 1984).

98 **The Way of Empathy**. This is an expanded version of a list of quotations found in *To the Peoples of the World: A Baha'i Statement on Peace* (The Association for Baha'i Studies, Ottawa, Canada 1986).

100 **The Book of Common Prayer**. See note 45. This blessing, which is given by the priest at the end of Holy Communion, echoes the words of St Paul in Philippians 4.7.

PUBLISHER'S ACKNOWLEDGEMENTS

We are grateful to the following for permission to reproduce copyright material:

Bloodaxe Books for the poem 'I will live and survive' from Irina Ratushinskaya (trans. David McDuff), *No, I'm Not Afraid* (Bloodaxe Books 1986).

Collins Publishers for an extract from Sheila Cassidy, *Prayer for Pilgrims* (Fount Paperbacks 1980).

Collins Publishers for a prayer from Alan Paton, *Instrument of Thy Peace* (Fount Paperbacks, 2nd edn 1983).

Darton Longman & Todd and St Vladimir's Seminary Press for an extract from Metropolitan Anthony and Georges Lefebvre, *Courage to Pray*, published and copyright 1984 by Darton Longman & Todd Ltd, London, and St Vladimir's Seminary Press.

The Executors of the Estate of C. Day Lewis for 'Will It Be So Again?' from his *Collected Poems* (Jonathan Cape 1954).

Harper & Row Publishers Inc. for an extract from James M. Washington, ed., *A Testament of Hope: The Essential Writings of Martin Luther King, Jr* (Harper & Row 1986).

Hartford Seminary, Connecticut, for an extract from A. J. Arberry, trans., 'A Poem of the Soul' in *The Muslim World*, vol. 30 (1940), 140–3.

Hodder & Stoughton for an extract from Mary Craig, *Candles in the Dark*, © 1984 by Mary Craig. Reprinted by permission of Hodder & Stoughton Ltd.

Hodder & Stoughton for an extract from Roy McKay, *John Leonard Wilson: Confessor for the Faith*, © 1973 by Roy McKay. Reprinted by permission of Hodder & Stoughton Ltd.

The Iona Community for the Celtic Benediction from the *Iona Community Worship Book* (Wild Goose Publications 1984).

Macmillan, London and Basingstoke, for a poem from *The Collected Poems and Plays of Rabindranath Tagore* (Macmillan 1916).

The Trustees of the Merton Legacy Trust for an extract from the 'Prayer for Peace' in Thomas Merton, *On Peace* (Mowbray 1976).

Reform Synagogues of Great Britain for two prayers from *Forms of Prayer for Jewish Worship, Daily Sabbath and Occasional Prayers*, 7th edn, © Reform Synagogues of Great Britain 1977.

SCM Press and Macmillan Publishing Co. for an extract from 'Night Voices in Tegel' in Dietrich Bonhoeffer, *Letters and Papers from Prison* (SCM, enlarged edn 1971; Macmillan 1972).

SCM Press and Harper and Row Publishers for an extract from John Macquarrie, *The Concept of Peace* (SCM and Harper and Row 1973).

Search Press for a poem from Ernesto Cardenal, *Psalms* (Sheed and Ward 1981).

Clifton Wolters for an extract from his translation of Julian of Norwich, *Revelations of Divine Love* (Penguin 1966).